بسم الله الرحمن الرحيم

# To The Reader

All the author's books explain faith-related issues in light of Qur'anic verses, and invite readers to learn God's words and to live by them. All the subjects concerning God's verses are explained so as to leave no doubt or room for questions in the reader's mind. The books' sincere, plain, and fluent style ensure that everyone of every age and from every social group can easily understand them. Thanks to their effective, lucid narrative, they can be read at a one sitting. Even those who rigorously reject spirituality are influenced by the facts these books document and cannot refute the truthfulness of their contents.

This and all the other books by the author can be read individually, or discussed in a group. Readers eager to profit from the books will find discussion very useful, letting them relate their reflections and experiences to one another.

In addition, it will be a great service to Islam to contribute to the publication and reading of these books, written solely for the pleasure of God. The author's books are all extremely convincing. For this reason, to communicate true religion to others, one of the most effective methods is encouraging them to read these books.

We hope the reader will look through the reviews of his other books at the back of this book. His rich source material on faith-related issues is very useful, and a pleasure to read.

In these books, unlike some other books, you will not find the author's personal views, explanations based on dubious sources, styles that are unobservant of the respect and reverence due to sacred subjects, nor hopeless, pessimistic arguments that create doubts in the mind and deviations in the heart.

# 24 Hours
## IN THE LIFE OF
## A MUSLIM

## HARUN YAHYA

Ta-Ha Publishers Ltd.
1 Wynne Road
London SW9 OBB
United Kingdom

# About The Author

Now writing under the pen-name of HARUN YAHYA, he was born in Ankara in 1956. Having completed his primary and secondary education in Ankara, he studied arts at Istanbul's Mimar Sinan University and philosophy at Istanbul University. Since the 1980s, he has published many books on political, scientific, and faith-related issues. Harun Yahya is well-known as the author of important works disclosing the imposture of evolutionists, their invalid claims, and the dark liaisons between Darwinism and such bloody ideologies as fascism and communism.

His penname is a composite of the names *Harun* (Aaron) and *Yahya* (John), in memory of the two esteemed Prophets who fought against their people's lack of faith. The Prophet's seal on the his books' covers is symbolic and is linked to the their contents. It represents the Qur'an (the final scripture) and the Prophet Muhammad (peace be upon him), last of the prophets. Under the guidance of the Qur'an and the Sunnah (teachings of the Prophet), the author makes it his purpose to disprove each fundamental tenet of godless ideologies and to have the "last word," so as to completely silence the objections raised against religion. He uses the seal of the final Prophet, who attained ultimate wisdom and moral perfection, as a sign of his intention to offer the last word.

All of Harun Yahya's works share one single goal: to convey the Qur'an's message, encourage readers to consider basic faith-related issues such as Allah's Existence and Unity and the Hereafter; and to expose godless systems' feeble foundations and perverted ideologies.

Harun Yahya enjoys a wide readership in many countries, from India to America, England to Indonesia, Poland to Bosnia, and Spain to Brazil. Some of his books are available in English, French, German, Spanish, Italian, Portuguese, Urdu, Arabic, Albanian, Russian, Serbo-Croat (Bosnian), Polish, Malay, Uygur Turkish, and Indonesian.

Greatly appreciated all around the world, these works have been instrumental in many people recovering faith in Allah and gaining deeper insights into their faith. His books' wisdom and sincerity, together with a distinct style that's easy to understand, directly affect anyone who reads them. Those who seriously consider these books, can no longer advocate atheism or any other perverted ideology or materialistic philosophy, since these books are characterized by rapid effectiveness, definite results, and irrefutability. Even if they continue to do so, it will be only a sentimental insistence, since these books refute such ideologies from their very foundations. All contemporary movements of denial are now ideologically defeated, thanks to the books written by Harun Yahya.

This is no doubt a result of the Qur'an's wisdom and lucidity. The author modestly intends to serve as a means in humanity's search for Allah's right path. No material gain is sought in the publication of these works.

Those who encourage others to read these books, to open their minds and hearts and guide them to become more devoted servants of Allah, render an invaluable service.

Meanwhile, it would only be a waste of time and energy to propagate other books that create confusion in people's minds, lead them into ideological chaos, and that clearly have no strong and precise effects in removing the doubts in people's hearts, as also verified from previous experience. It is impossible for books devised to emphasize the author's literary power rather than the noble goal of saving people from loss of faith, to have such a great effect. Those who doubt this can readily see that the sole aim of Harun Yahya's books is to overcome disbelief and to disseminate the Qur'an's moral values. The success and impact of this service are manifested in the readers' conviction.

One point should be kept in mind: The main reason for the continuing cruelty, conflict, and other ordeals endured by the vast majority of people is the ideological prevalence of disbelief. This can be ended only with the ideological defeat of disbelief and by conveying the wonders of creation and Qur'anic morality so that people can live by it. Considering the state of the world today, leading into a downward spiral of violence, corruption and conflict, clearly this service must be provided speedily and effectively, or it may be too late.

In this effort, the books of Harun Yahya assume a leading role. By the will of Allah, these books will be a means through which people in the twentyfirst century will attain the peace, justice, and happiness promised in the Qur'an.

The works of the author include *The New Masonic Order, Judaism and Freemasonry, Global*

Freemasonry, The Kabbala and Freemasonry, The Knight Templars, Templars and Freemasonry, Israel's Policy of World Domination, Islam Denounces Terrorism, The Black Clan, Terrorism: The Ritual of the Devil, The Disasters Darwinism Brought to Humanity, Communism in Ambush, Fascism: The Bloody Ideology of Darwinism, The 'Secret Hand' in Bosnia, Behind the Scenes of Terrorism, Israel's Kurdish Card, Communist China's Policy of Oppression in East Turkestan, Palestine, Solution: The Values of the Qur'an, The Winter of Islam and The Spring to Come, Islam and Buddhism, The Philosophy of Zionism, Articles 1-2-3, Romanticism: A Weapon of Satan, The Light of the Qur'an Has Destroyed Satanism, Signs From the Chapter of the Cave in the Qur'an to the Last Times, The End Times and the Mahdi, Signs From the Qur'an, Signs of the Last Day, The Last Times and The Beast of the Earth, Truths 1-2, Idealism The Philosophy of Matrix and the True Nature of Matter, The Western World Turns to God, The Evolution Deceit, The Perfect Design in the Universe Is Not by Chance, Why Darwinism Is Incompatable with the Qur'an, Darwinism Refuted, New Research Demolishes Evolution, A Definitive Reply to Evolutionist Propaganda, The Quandary of Evolution I-II (Encyclopedic), The Error of the Evolution of Species, The Blunders of Evolutionists, The Collapse of the Theory of Evolution in 50 Steps, The Errors of The NAS: A Reply to the National Academy of Sciences Booklet Science and Creationism, Confessions of Evolutionists, Perished Nations, For Men of Understanding, Love of Allah, Allah's Art of Affection, The Glad Tidings of the Messiah, The Prophet Musa (as), The Prophet Yusuf (as), The Prophet Muhammad (saas), The Prophet Sulayman (as), The Prophet Ibrahim (as) and the Prophet Lut (as), Maryam (as) The Exemplary Muslim Woman, The Golden Age, Allah Exists, Allah's Artistry in Colour, Magnificence Everywhere, The Importance of the Evidences of Creation, The Truth of the Life of This World, The Nightmare of Disbelief, Knowing the Truth, Eternity Has Already Begun, Timelessness and the Reality of Fate, Matter: Another Name for Illusion, The Little Man in the Tower, Islam and Karma, The Dark Magic of Darwinism, The Religion of Darwinism, The Collapse of the Theory of Evolution in 20 Questions, Allah is Known Through Reason, The Qur'an Leads the Way to Science, Consciousness in the Cell, Biomimetics Technology Imitates Nature, The Engineering in Nature, A String of Miracles, The Creation of the Universe, Miracles of the Qur'an, The Design in Nature, Self-Sacrifice and Intelligent Behaviour Models in Animals, Deep Thinking, Never Plead Ignorance, The Green Miracle: Photosynthesis, The Miracle in the Cell, The Miracle in the Eye, The Miracle in the Spider, The Miracle in the Mosquito, The Miracle in the Ant, The Miracle of the Immune System, The Miracle of Creation in Plants, The Miracle in the Atom, The Miracle in the Honeybee, The Miracle of Seed, The Miracle of Hormones, The Miracle of the Termite, The Miracle of the Human Body, The Miracle of Human Creation, The Miracle of Protein, The Miracle of Smell and Taste, The Miracle of the Microworld, The Secrets of DNA, The Miracle in the Molecule, The Miracle of Creation in DNA, The Miracle of Talking Birds.

The author's childrens books are: Wonders of Allah's Creation, The World of Animals, The Glory in the Heavens, Wonderful Creatures, Let's Learn Our Islam, The World of Our Little Friends: The Ants, Honeybees That Build Perfect Combs, Skillful Dam Constructors: Beavers, Tell Me About Creation, The Miracle in Our Body, A Day in the Life of a Muslim, Children This is for You I-II

The author's other works on Quranic topics include: The Basic Concepts in the Qur'an, The Moral Values of the Qur'an, Quick Grasp of Faith 1-2-3, Ever Thought About the Truth?, Crude Understanding of Disbelief, Devoted to Allah, Abandoning the Society of Ignorance, Paradise: The Believers' Real Home, Learning from the Qur'an, An Index to the Qur'an, Emigrating for the Cause of Allah, The Character of the Hypocrite in the Qur'an, The Secrets of the Hypocrite, Names of Allah, Communicating the Message and Disputing in the Qur'an, Answers from the Qur'an, Death Resurrection Hell, The Struggle of the Messengers, The Avowed Enemy of Man: Satan, The Greatest Slander: Idolatry, The Religion of the Ignorant, The Arrogance of Satan, Prayer in the Qur'an, The Theory of Evolution, The Importance of Conscience in the Qur'an, The Day of Resurrection, Never Forget, Commonly Disregarded Qur'anic Rulings, Human Characters in the Society of Ignorance, The Importance of Patience in the Qur'an, Perfected Faith, Before You Regret, Our Messengers Say, The Mercy of Believers, The Fear of Allah, Jesus Will Return, Beauties for Life in the Qur'an, A Bouquet of the Beauties of Allah 1-2-3-4, The Iniquity Called "Mockery," The Mystery of the Test, Real Wisdom Described in the Qur'an, The Struggle Against the Religion of Irreligion, The School of Yusuf, The Alliance of the Good, Slanders Spread Against Muslims Throughout History, The Importance of Following the Good Word, Why Do You Deceive Yourself?, Islam: The Religion of Ease, Zeal and Enthusiasm Described in the Qur'an, Seeing Good in All, How do the Unwise Interpret the Qur'an?, Some Secrets of the Qur'an, The Courage of Believers, Hopefulness in the Qur'an, Justice and Tolerance in the Qur'an, Basic Tenets of Islam, Those Who do not Heed the Qur'an, Taking the Qur'an as a Guide, A Lurking Threat: Heedlessness, Sincerity Described in the Qur'an, The Happiness of Believers, Those Who Exhaust Their Pleasures During Their Wordly Lives, A Sly Game of Satan, Passivism in Religion, The Religion of Worshipping People, Agonies of a Fake World, How a Muslim Speaks, The Silent Language of Evil, The Ruses of the Liar in the Qur'an, Loyalty in the Qur'an, The Solution to Secret Torments.

Copyright© Harun Yahya 1424 AH / 2003 CE
First published by Vural Yayincilik, Istanbul, Turkey in April 2003

Published by:
Ta-Ha Publishers Ltd.
1 Wynne Road
London SW9 OBB
United Kingdom

Website: http://www.taha.co.uk
E-mail: sales@taha.co.uk

All translations from the Qur'an are from
"The Noble Qur'an: a New Rendering of its Meaning in English"
by Hajj Abdalhaqq an Aisha Bewley,
published by Bookwork, Norwich, UK. 1420 CE/1999 AH

By Harun Yahya
Translated by Ron Evans
Edited by Abdassamad Clarke

A Catalog Record of this book is available from the British Library
ISBN 184200054 3

Printed and bound by: SEÇİL OFSET - November 2003
100 Yıl Mahallesi MAS-SİT Matbaacılar Sitesi
4. Cadde No: 77 Bağcılar-İstanbul Tel: (0 212) 629 06 15

www.harunyahya.com

# contents

# Introduction

In the Qur'an, Allah Himself responds to all the questions a person needs answered throughout his life and provides the perfect and most rational solutions for all problems that arise. As Allah says in the second verse of Surat al-Baqara, **"That is the Book, without any doubt. It contains guidance for those who guard against evil."** Other verses also show that our Lord has explained everything in the Qur'an:

> There is instruction in their stories for people of intelligence. This is not a narration which has been invented but confirmation of all that came before, a clarification of everything, and a guidance and a mercy for people who believe. (Surah Yusuf: 111)

**… We have sent down the Book to you making all things clear and as guidance and mercy and good news for the Muslims. (Surah an-Nahl: 89)**

A person of faith orders his whole life according to the Qur'an and strives to apply carefully from day to day what he has read and learned in its verses. In everything he does from the moment he gets up in the morning until the time he falls asleep at night, he is intent on thinking, speaking and acting according to the teachings of the Qur'an. Allah shows in the Qur'an that this dedication dominates the whole life of a believer.

**Say: "My prayer and my rites, my living and my dying, are for Allah alone, the Lord of all the worlds." (Surat al-An'am: 162)**

But some people think that religion is composed of rituals limited to certain times—that life is divided into times for prayer and other times. They think about Allah and the afterlife only when they pray, fast, give sadaqah or go on the pilgrimage to Makkah. At other times they are engrossed in the business of the world. Life in this world is for them an unpleasant rat-race. Such people are almost totally divorced from the Qur'an and have their own personal goals in life, their own understanding of morality, their own worldview and sense of values. The have no idea of what the teaching of the Qur'an really means.

A person who adopts the teaching of the Qur'an and follows the Sunnah of the Messenger of Allah, may Allah bless him and grant him peace, as his principle of living will certainly live life quite differently from someone with this mentality. Such a person will not forget that he is subject to the destiny that Allah has decreed for him and will live his life trusting in, and submitting to, Him. Therefore, he will know that he must not be anxious, sad, fearful, worried, pessimistic or depressed; or overtaken by panic in the face of difficulties. He will meet everything that comes along in the way that Allah advises and approves. His every word, decision and action show that he lives according to the Sunnah which is the practical embodiment of the teaching of the Qur'an. Whether he is taking a walk, eating a meal, going to school, studying, working, playing sports, having a conversation, watching television or listening to music, he is aware that he is responsible for living his life according to the what is pleasing to Allah. He takes care of matters with which he has been entrusted meticulously and is concerned at the same time to win Allah's favour in the things he does. He never behaves in a way unbefitting the teaching of the Qur'an or contrary to the Sunnah.

Living by the values of Islam is possible by applying the commands and advice given in the Qur'an to every aspect of life. This and the practice of the Sunnah is the only way that people can achieve the best and happiest results in this world and the next. Our Lord tells us in the Qur'an that a person can attain the best kind of life by doing right actions:

**Anyone who acts rightly, male or female, being a believer, We will give them a good life and We will recompense them according to the best of what they did. (Surat an-Nahl: 97)**

By Allah's will, living according to the teaching of the Qur'an and the Sunnah will enable people to develop a broad way of understanding, superior intelligence, the ability to distinguish right from wrong and the ability to consider a matter in depth. These characteristics will ensure that the person who possesses them will live every moment of his life in the ease that comes from these advantages. A person who lives his life in submission to Allah and according to the teaching of the Qur'an will be totally different from other people how he behaves, sits and walks, in his point of view and how he explains and interprets things, and in the solutions he finds for the problems that confront him.

This book will examine the things a person does and the events he encounters almost every day of his life from the point of view of a Muslim who lives according to the teachings of the Qur'an. It will show how a Muslim should react to the various daily events and situations with which he is faced. The purpose of the book is twofold: to present an idea of the good life that can be had thanks to the teaching of the Qur'an, and to invite all people into the superior life offered by this teaching. It is certain that only the teaching of the Qur'an makes it possible for a person to live every hour of every day, and every moment of his life in a Paradise-like, peaceful environment far from the stress, worry and anxiety of this world.

# Chapter 1

## 24 HOURS IN THE LIFE OF A MUSLIM ACCORDING TO THE TEACHINGS OF THE QUR'AN

## Waking up in the morning

One of the basic differences between Muslims who live their lives according to the teachings of the Qur'an and those people who reject Allah is this: the wisdom Allah gives to those who use their conscience and stand in awe of the glory of Allah. (For a detailed discussion see Harun Yahya's *True Wisdom Described in The Qur'an*) Because of their wisdom, believers are immediately aware of the reason behind events that godless people and those unable to grasp the truth regard as meaningless happenstance.

From the moment a believer wakes up in the morning, he knows that there is (as Allah calls them in the Qur'an), a "sign" in every experience he has in the course of a day. The word "sign" is given to those events in existence that are clear proofs of the existence, unity and the attributes of Allah—and it is also the name for a verse of the Qur'an. Another idea similar in meaning is "the facts that lead to faith." This may be defined as those facts that bring a person to faith, and at the same time cause faith to grow, develop and become strong. But only those who sincerely turn to Allah can recognise these "signs" and facts that lead to faith. The 190th verse of Surah Al 'Imran is an example of this:

> **In the creation of the heavens and the earth, and the alternation of night and day, there are Signs for people with intelligence. (Surah Al 'Imran: 190)**

For those who have faith and live by the teachings of the Qur'an, every new day is full of proofs of Allah's existence and facts leading to faith. For example, to open one's eyes and start the day is one of Allah's blessings to humanity and one of the facts leading to faith that needs to be pondered. This is because a person is unconscious throughout the night and all he can remember from those long hours of sleep are some indistinct dreams that last 3-5 seconds. During this time, a person is asleep with no connection to this world.

His body and his spirit part company, and this time, during which he thinks he is sleeping, is actually a kind of death. Allah reveals in the Qur'an that human selves are taken while they are asleep.

**Allah takes back people's selves when their death arrives and those who have not yet died, while they are asleep. He keeps hold of those whose death has been decreed and sends the others back for a specified term... (Surat az-Zumar: 42)**

**It is He Who takes you back to Himself at night, while knowing the things you perpetrate by day, and then wakes you up again, so that a specified term may be fulfilled. (Surat al-An'am: 60)**

In these verses, Allah says that human selves are taken during sleep, but are given back again until the determined hour of death comes. While asleep, a person partly loses consciousness of the outside world. To awake from the "death" of sleep to consciousness and the same condition as the day before, and to be able to see, hear and feel perfectly well is a miracle that we should consider. A person who goes to bed at night cannot be certain that these incomparable blessings will be given to him again in the morning. And we can never be sure if we will meet with some kind of disaster or wake up in a healthy state.

A believer starting a new day thinks about these facts and thanks Allah for covering him with His great mercy and protection. He

looks at the new day as an opportunity given him by Allah to win His pleasure and gain Paradise. The moment he opens his eyes in the morning of the early dawn, he directs his thoughts to Allah and begins the day with a sincere prayer, the dawn prayer of Islam.

During the day, he acts with the knowledge that Allah is always watching him, and is careful to win His approval by obeying His commands and counsel. He established a close bond with Allah and began the day with the dawn prayer. In this way, the likelihood that he will forget Allah's good pleasure during the day or ignore His limits is small; he will behave throughout the day with the knowledge that Allah is testing him in this world.

Someone who sincerely directs his thoughts to Allah will be helped to see that he must think carefully about the blessings he has been given and that no one other than Allah has the power to give them to him.

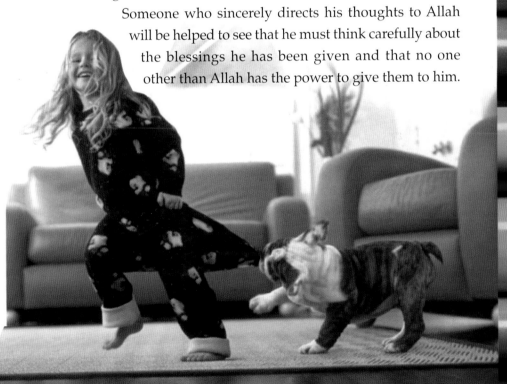

In the Qur'an, our Lord says that people must ponder this matter:

> **Say: "What do you think? If Allah took away your hearing and your sight and sealed up your hearts, what god is there, other than Allah, who could give them back to you?" (Surat al-An'am: 46)**

Certainly it is the Almighty and All-Knowing Allah Who makes sleep a time of rest for human beings and restores His blessings to them in the morning. Those who know this feel Allah's proximity from the moment they begin their day and are pleased with the incomparable blessings they enjoy.

Those who reject religion and refuse to consider this reality can never be fully aware of the blessings they have or know the joy that believers experience. Generally, early in the morning, they find it difficult to get out of a warm bed and are stressed by the anxiety of having to get into step with the new day. Some are anxious and depressed because of the things they have to do every morning. They don't want to get out of bed; there is a struggle in their minds between getting up and having one more minute of sleep. An often encountered moral failing in these kinds of people is that they are irritable, stressed and glum when they wake up.

Godless people cannot enjoy the pleasure of Allah's blessings; from the moment they wake up in the morning they return to the monotony of doing the same things every day. There is another kind of person who is unaware that the new day may be the last opportunity Allah has given him: he prepares himself quickly to start his day avid to make more money, to show off to others with his

possessions or appearance, to attract the attention of others and be liked.

Those who ignore the facts that Allah has revealed in the Qur'an may start their day in their own ways, but there is a common lack of wisdom in the way they behave: they do not consider that Allah created them, that they are responsible for serving Him and winning His approval and that the new day before them may be the last opportunity they have to fulfil their duty towards Him. Allah reveals their condition in these words:

> **Mankind's Reckoning has drawn very close to them, yet they heedlessly turn away. (Surat al-Anbiya': 1)**

It is clear that those who live immersed in this great error have made a huge mistake. One must not forget that every morning may be the beginning of the last day allotted to one's earthly life. Death may come at any moment, because of a traffic accident, an unexpected disease or any one of countless other causes. In that case, as we said above, we must think about what we have to do to spend the day before us so as to win Allah's approval.

# Cleaning

There are some reasons for the changes that happen to your body when you wake up in the morning. Your face swells, your hair is dirty, your body has an unpleasant odour and there is an unwelcome taste in your mouth. The swollen face you see in the mirror and your unkempt appearance show you just how dependent you are. Everyone must wash their face in the morning, brush their teeth and groom himself or herself. This reminds someone who has espoused the teaching of the Qur'an that in this he is no different from other people, and that only Allah has no imperfections.

Moreover, when someone who sincerely turns to Allah looks in the mirror and feels uncomfortable at what he sees, he understands better that he cannot possess anything of beauty by the power of his own will.

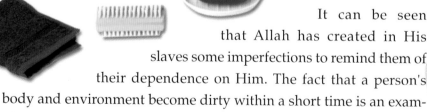

It can be seen that Allah has created in His slaves some imperfections to remind them of their dependence on Him. The fact that a person's body and environment become dirty within a short time is an example of this. But Allah has shown people how to overcome these imperfections and has made blessings such as soap and detergent available to us. Allah shows this to us in the Qur'an:

**For truly with hardship comes ease; truly with hardship comes ease. (Surat al-Inshirah: 5-6)**

The ability to notice this secret of the creation of blessings and to give thanks for them to Allah belongs only to believers endowed with understanding.

While a believer cleans himself, in the morning or in the course of the day, he gives thanks that Allah has provided the materials with which to do it. Because he knows that Allah loves cleanliness and clean people, he sees washing himself as an act of worship and hopes to gain His pleasure. He gladly obeys what Allah has commanded in verses 4 and 5 of Surat al-Muddaththir:

**Purify your clothes. Shun all filth. (Surat al-Muddaththir: 4-5)**

In the following verse revealed about events during the battle of Badr, Allah says that He sends down water from the heavens for people to clean themselves and for their other needs.

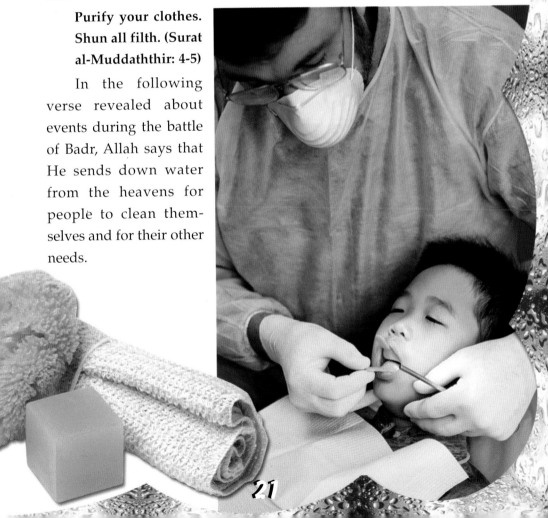

21

**And when He overcame you with sleep, making you feel secure, and sent you down water from heaven to purify you and remove the taint of Shaytan from you, and to fortify your hearts and make your feet firm. (Surat al-Anfal: 11)**

Water is the basic requirement needed for people to clean their bodies, their possessions and their houses. Besides being able to clean visible dirt and invisible bacteria, water also has the ability to help one relax. When water pours over the body, it can disperse the static electricity that makes people fatigued and out of sorts. We can't see the static electricity produced on our bodies, but it sometimes makes itself noticeable by a crackling sound when we take off our sweaters, a mild electric shock when we touch something or by the movement of our hair. When we wash ourselves, we rid ourselves of this accumulation of static electricity and our bodies feel light and comfortable as a result. The freshness of the air after rain has fallen also comes from the fact that water has cleaned the air of static electricity.

Allah is pleased when people are clean and well-groomed. This can be seen in a few verses in the Qur'an that allude to the physical cleanliness of people in the Garden.

Allah says that **"… there will be youths like hidden pearls."** (Surat at-Tur: 24), and in other verses Allah says that there are **"purified wives"** for those in the Garden. (Surat al-Baqara: 25; Surah Al 'Imran: 15; Surat an-Nisa': 57)

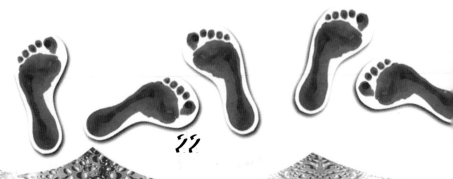

Some people give importance to being well-groomed only when they are with others or when they have to make themselves liked; they don't care about their appearance and their cleanliness when they are not in the presence of others. To find it normal to go around the house until evening unwashed

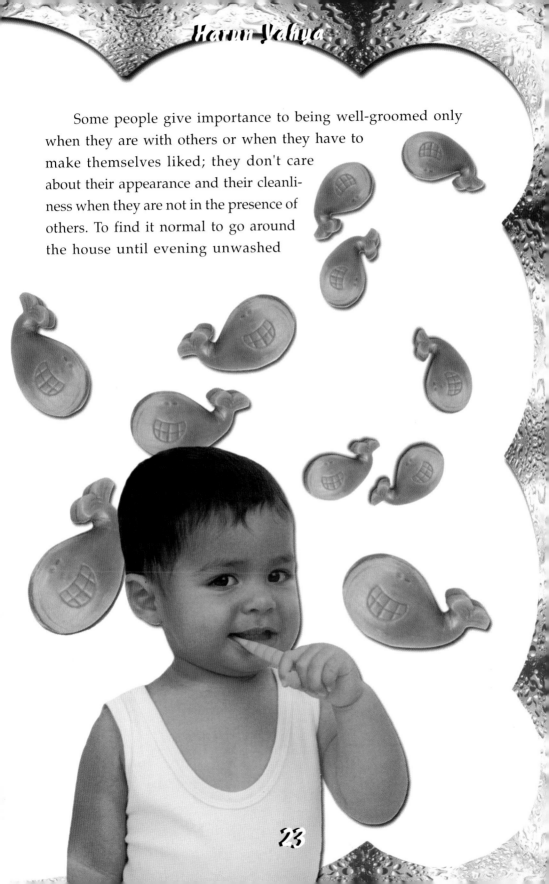

with a dirty face and bad breath, ungroomed, with the bed unmade and untidy room is the result of faulty reasoning.

However, Allah urges Muslims to make the best and cleanest environments for themselves and commands everyone to maintain the utmost cleanliness in everything from food and clothing to the places in which they live.

**Mankind! Eat what is good and lawful on the earth. (Surat al-Baqara: 168)**

**They will ask you what is lawful for them. Say: "All good things are lawful for you..." (Surat al-Ma'ida: 4)**

**... (The Prophet) commanding them to do right and forbidding them to do wrong, making good things lawful for them and bad things unlawful for them... (Surat al-A'raf: 157)**

**And when We made the House a place of return, a sanctuary for mankind: They took the Maqam of Ibrahim**

as a place of prayer. We contracted with Ibrahim and Isma'il: "Purify My House for those who circle it, and those who stay there, and those who bow and who prostrate." (Surat al-Baqara: 125)

They replied, "We have been here for a day or part of a day." They said, "Your Lord knows best how long you have been here. Send one of your number into the city with this silver you have, so he can see which food is purest and bring you some of it to eat." (Surat al-Kahf: 19)

And tenderness and purity from Us, he (Yahya) had taqwa (i.e., consciousness of Allah that leads one to obey Him and not disobey Him). (Surah Maryam: 13)

While the lifestyle of ignorant people leads them to make uncomfortable and unhealthy environments to live in with their own hands, Muslims, in conformity with the teachings of the Qur'an, live a good life in this world. Ignorant people create environments that are troublesome both for themselves and those around them, while Muslims lead their lives in healthy, invigorating places where everyone can live in comfort and peace of mind.

In short, in conformity with the teachings of the Qur'an, believers will be clean and well-groomed, not for the sake of other people, but because this is what Allah likes and, naturally, because this is what feels most comfortable. By cleaning the place where they live, they feel a great deal of pleasure from creating an environment in which other people feel comfortable; in the matter of cleanliness they don't show the least laxity and they always do everything in their power to be clean and well-groomed.

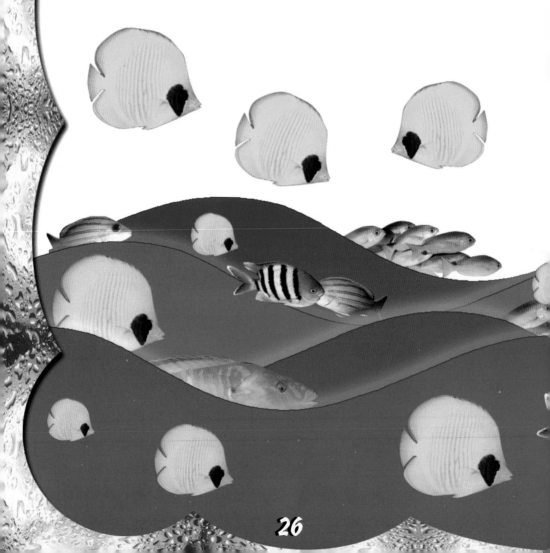

## Dressing

While a believer decides on what clothes he is going to wear during the day and gets dressed, he is aware of an important fact: that clothing is one of Allah's countless blessings and there is good reason for its existence. Everyone benefits from this blessing, but only a Muslim who lives according to the teaching of the Qur'an properly appreciates that beautiful clothing is a mercy from Allah and thanks Him for it. Clothing immediately reminds the believer that living things are the source of wool, cotton and silk clothing. The articles of clothing we use, almost every moment of our lives, are obtained from plants and animals that are wonders of creation. In other words, if Allah had not created some living things with the ability to provide human beings with every kind of clothing from the most basic to the most luxurious, these raw materials would not exist.

Despite the fact that they know this, some people either ignore it or, because of the error of their ways, don't appreciate the blessings they have. Because they were given the clothes they need from the minute they were born, dressing has become a habit for them. This habit prevents them from realising that their clothing is a blessing and from giving thanks for it. But one of the reasons why our Lord created blessings in this word is that human beings would thank Him for them. So, let's examine the reasons why Allah created clothing for us beginning with the benefits it provides us.

Clothing is like a shield that protects the human body from cold, the dangerous rays of the sun and minor dangers such as cuts and bruises from our environment. If we didn't have clothing, the thin skin that covers the human body would often be injured by these kinds of small accidents. They are painful, a threat to health

and the skin could take on a very bad appearance.

Our Lord in the Qur'an reveals another reason behind the creation of protective clothing:

**Children of Adam! We have sent down clothing to you to conceal your private parts, and fine apparel. (Surat al-A'raf: 26)**

As this verse point out, clothing gives human beings a much better appearance aesthetically.

It is clear that clothing is an indispensable need and an extremely important blessing that Allah has provided for our use. A believer who is aware of this will be very careful and fastidious in the use of his clothing, and this will be an indication that he is truly thankful to Allah for the blessings he has been given.

Another quality given to the believer from the values taught by the Qur'an is moderation in spending money and this applies also when buying clothing. He buys items that he needs, that

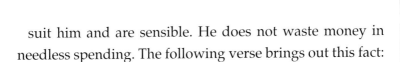

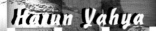

suit him and are sensible. He does not waste money in needless spending. The following verse brings out this fact:

**Those who, when they spend, are neither extravagant nor mean, but take a stance mid way between the two. (Surat al-Furqan: 67)**

The care with which a person living according to the teachings of the Qur'an dresses is not limited to this. For example, besides dressing in clean clothes, a believer with a sense of values will be careful to dress as well and as suitably for the occasion as possible. As the Qur'an shows, clothing is pleasing to the eye (Surat al-A'raf: 26). There are examples of how our Prophet, may Allah bless him and grant him peace, dressed and his recommendations on this matter in the sayings that have come down to us:

"Eat what you like, and wear what you like provided that it is free from two things: extravagance and vainglory." *(Maulana Muhammad Manzoor No'mani, Ma'ariful Hadith)*

And here is another bit of information that has come down to us about how our Prophet, may Allah bless him and grant him peace, dressed:

**Whenever a delegation came to meet the Messenger of Allah, he would wear his best clothes and order his leading Companions to do likewise." (*Tabaqat Hadith*, Volume 4, Number 346)**

When one of his companions gave no importance to his appearance and seemed unkempt, our Prophet, may Allah bless him and grant him peace, warned him immediately. An example of this has been passed down to us:

**"The Messenger of Allah was in the mosque, when a man with unkempt hair and an untidy beard came in. The Prophet (saas) pointed to him, as if indicating to him that he should tidy up his hair and beard. The man went and did so, then returned. The Prophet (saas) said, 'Is this not better than that any one of you should come with unkempt hair?'" (*Malik's Muwatta*,**

Volume 2, Number 949)

In the Qur'an, Allah says that clothing and adornments will be among the finest blessings of the Garden. Some of them are mentioned in the following verses:

**But Allah will admit those who believe and do right actions into Gardens with rivers flowing under them where they will be adorned with gold bracelets and pearls, and where their clothing will be of silk. (Surat al-Hajj: 23)**

**Wearing fine silk and rich brocade, face to face with one another. (Surat ad-Dukhan: 53)**

**They will wear green garments of fine silk and rich brocade. They will be adorned with silver bracelets... (Surat al-Insan: 21)**

In these verses, our Lord speaks of robes of silk and rich brocade, and adornments made of gold, silver and pearls. The adornments we have in this world are similar to those in the Garden, and for a person of faith, seeing these adornments—whether he possesses any or not—is a means that leads him to contemplate the Garden and desire even more to go there. A believer sees the purpose of these things in creation and realises that all the blessings of

this world are transitory. The only real blessings and those that will last forever are in the afterlife.

> But as for those who believe and do right actions, We will not let the wage of good-doers go to waste. They will have Gardens of Eden with rivers flowing under them. They will be adorned in them with bracelets made of gold and wear green garments made of the finest silk and rich brocade, reclining there on couches under canopies. What an excellent reward! What a wonderful repose! (Surat al-Kahf: 30-31)

One of the things a person living according to the

teachings of the Qur'an and the Sunnah must consider about clothing is that outer appearance is very important when establishing relationships with other people. For this reason, a believer will give even more attention to what he wears when he invites people to accept the deen (religion) of the Qur'an. He will be as eager as possible to dress in clean clothes that are modest and suitable for him. This shows that he has a devout regard for the commands of Allah and respect for other people.

Only those who live according to the teachings of the Qur'an are as considerate of a person's psychological state and careful to be as effective as possible in telling that person about eternal salvation as they are meticulous about what they wear.

In conclusion, a person of faith, taking our Prophet, may Allah bless him and grant him peace, as his example, always goes about in clean, well cared-for and attractive clothes; he or she takes pleasure in this and by it hopes to win Allah's approval.

## Breakfast

Every believer to whom Allah has given the ability to think and understand knows when he goes into the kitchen to make breakfast in the morning that all the blessings of food and drink given in creation are facts leading to faith.

For example, the fire he uses to cook his food can cause a great deal of harm to him as well as to many other things; it also has the ability to destroy. But heat is a requirement for making food edible and from this point of view it is a very great blessing. In other words, like everything else on the earth, fire has been put at the service of human beings. In the Qur'an, Allah says,

**And He has made everything in the heavens and everything on the earth subservient to you. (Surat al-Jathiyya: 13)**

Besides this, fire is a reminder for the believer in this life of the pains of the Fire. In describing in the Qur'an those who will go

to Hell, Allah mentions a violent fire. In a few verses, He describes the pains of the fire He has created for those who reject Him:

**On the Day they are tormented by the Fire. (Surat adh-Dhariyat: 13)**

**The Fire will sear their faces, making them grimace horribly in it, their lips drawn back from their teeth. (Surat al-Muminun: 104)**

**Whoever does not believe in Allah and His Messenger, We have prepared a Blazing Fire for the disbelievers. (Surat al-Fath: 13)**

When believers with a profound faith think of this raging fire of Hell, their fear of Allah grows, they pray to Him and take refuge in Him from the Hellfire. In this way very small everyday things serve as reminders of major matters, and this is a very important part of the practice of the believer.

A person who thinks sincerely and without prejudice about the food we eat for

breakfast will find many reminders in it. The taste and smell of bread, honey, cheese, tomatoes, tea and fruitjuice, their food value and various colours are all blessings. They all provide the proteins, amino acids, carbohydrates, fats, vitamins, minerals and fluids that the body needs. To live a healthy life, we have to be regularly and properly nourished, but this is not a difficult chore for us; it's something we enjoy. Fruits, vegetables, cereals, and pasta meet a person's every need for nourishment and also give him a lot of pleasure.

Actually, all that we have mentioned are really small items that everyone knows very well and has lived intimately with every 24 hours since he was born. But most people don't consider these things correctly that our Lord has given for our daily use. They take them all for granted and don't realise just how valuable they are.

But all this delicious food and drink has the ability to

provide various benefits to the human body, and each of them is a wonder of creation. For example, a bee weighing only a few grams produces honey. Both because of the vitamins and minerals it contains and the structural characteristics it has, honey means health and healing for human beings. In the Qur'an Allah says that He inspired this quality of honey and the physical work of the honeybee:

> Your Lord revealed to the bees: "Build dwellings in the mountains and the trees, and also in the structures which men erect. Then eat from every kind of fruit and travel the paths of your Lord, which have been made easy for you to follow." From inside them comes a drink of varying colours, containing healing for mankind. There is certainly a Sign in that for people who reflect. (Surat an-Nahl: 68-69)

A believer who considers the production of honey becomes aware of the miracle of creation that it contains. He immediately understands that neither the blossoms of fruit trees, which provide the basic raw material for honey, and whose nectar the bees turn into honey, nor the wonderful honey itself, could happen by chance. And this brings him closer to Allah.

In addition, the absolute obedience of a tiny bee to our Lord is another fact leading to faith. The believer will understand that it is by Allah's inspiration that the honeybee, with neither intelligence nor consciousness as we understand them, works unceasingly and

with perfect discipline to perform its wonderful functions.

The importance of the meat, milk, cheese, and other animal products as blessings for humanity from Allah is announced in the Qur'an:

> **And there is certainly a lesson for you in your livestock. We give you to drink from what is in their bellies and there are many ways in which you benefit from them, and some of them you eat. (Surat al-Muminun: 21)**

And there is mention of **"what is in their bellies"**, while informing us of the benefits we get from animals. For example, there is something left over in the digestive process from the food a cow has eaten, the water it has drunk, the blood circulating in its veins and its internal organs. It is indeed a miracle that a sweet-smelling, clean, white mixture like milk that is so beneficial to human health could come from such a complex mixture. Besides this, it is produced in the healthiest conditions despite the fact that it is located in an area containing waste material.

Another indication of Allah's supreme knowledge is the fact that the only raw material that goes into making white milk is green grass. But milk-producing animals create a white liq-

uid from a stiff, green material thanks to a wonderful system that Allah has created in their bodies. In the Qur'an, our Lord tells us what milk is made of:

**There is instruction for you in cattle. From the contents of their bellies, from between the dung and blood, We give you pure milk to drink, easy for drinkers to swallow. (Surat an-Nahl: 66)**

As we know, milk is a very rich food containing several materials that the human body needs; it is a liquid that plays a vital role in the nourishment of both children and adults.

Another food that comes from animals, small in itself but with high nutritional value, is the egg. The formation of this storehouse of proteins, vitamins and minerals is another miracle. A chicken with little awareness produces eggs every day and protects the eggs it has produced with a wonderful wrapping.

To consider how an eggshell is so won-

derfully formed around the fluid inside it or how the fluid has been placed inside the shell although it has no cover, increases the wonder that a believer feels at the creative artistry of Allah.

Various drinks, which some consider indispensable for breakfast, come from plants. After the leaves of these plants have been put through certain processes, they become sweet-smelling liquids. The thousands of other kinds of plants that grow in the same soil display the endless power, knowledge and mercy of Allah Who created them. As our Lord says in the Qur'an:

**It is He Who produces gardens, both cultivated and wild, and palm-trees and crops of diverse kinds, and olives and pomegranates, both similar and dissimilar... (Surat al-An`am: 141)**

Allah gives us countless blessings that He has created for us to eat. He tests human beings in this earthly life with wealth and poverty, He is pleased with those who display fine moral qualities when confronted by these tests and He reveals in the Qur'an that they will receive the endless blessings of the Garden. For example, some people eat a fine breakfast while others have only a few bits of food. But a believer, whether or not he is prosperous, will always behave in a manner so as to win Allah's approval and will give thanks to Him with all sincerity. If he is rich, he will not boast or become arrogant. If he is poor, he

will not feel anxious or sorry for himself.

A believer is aware that Allah is putting him through a test and that everything in this life is transitory. The Qur'an says that Allah will test human beings with good and evil. **"We test you with both good and evil as a trial. And you will be returned to Us."** (Surat al-Anbiya': 35) For this reason, a person who lives according to the teachings of the Qur'an knows that it is not the blessings that he has received but his attitude towards those blessings that will win him a reward in Allah's sight. Even if he is not prosperous, a believer will sincerely give thanks to Allah. In the Qur'an, Allah reveals that He will increase the blessings of those who give thanks with sincerity and determination and reminds the ungrateful that the pains of Hell are terrible:

And when your Lord announced: "If you are grateful, I will certainly give you increase, but if you are ungrateful, My punishment is severe."
**(Surah Ibrahim: 7)**

Someone who considers the proofs of the perfect creation around him, as well as the reasons for food, will also see the divine intentions in the structure and working of the mouth created to eat these things easily. In order for a human being to eat, his food, his lips, teeth, tongue, jaw, saliva glands and millions of cells work together in perfect harmony. This is all perfectly orchestrated such that several functions can be performed at the same time without a hitch. The teeth bite the food into pieces and the tongue continually pushes it between the teeth to be chewed. With its strong muscles, the jaw helps the teeth to chew while the eater moves the tongue in an appropriate manner. The lips act as a securely closed door to prevent food from falling out of the mouth.

Besides this, the parts that make up these organs work together in perfect harmony. For example, the teeth, according to their location and structure, bite the food into pieces and chew it. All the teeth are ordered and arranged in their places according to their function; every one of them grows and stays a certain length in order to work cooperatively with the tooth opposite it. Certainly these organs have no consciousness or intelligence; they cannot decide among themselves to cooperate with one another. And the excellent organisation briefly described above cannot come about randomly. Every part is made exactly as required to achieve a certain goal. There is no doubt that this marvellous design is from our Lord Who **"created everything and determined it most exactly."** (Surat al-Furqan: 2). Allah has created all of these things in order to make it easy for human beings to eat their food and take benefit and pleasure from it.

Another important thing on which a believer reflects is the fact that he can perceive the smells of the food in the kitchen and can taste it without any effort. This is possible because of the wonderful faculties he has. His sense of taste and smell, which do not cease throughout his life, work perfectly for him at no cost; they have taken no training to work so effectively and are themselves unconscious of their workings.

If a person did not have his sense of taste, the various tastes of meat, fish, vegetables, soups, salads, fruits, drinks, and jams would have no meaning for him. Besides, the taste of these things might not be good; they might be tasteless, insipid and unpleasant and upset the stomach. There is no doubt that tastes and the faculty that perceives them have been specially

created for human beings. It would be a big mistake to be unaware of this because of the insensitivity created by habit. The Qur'an reveals that Allah created good and clean food for human beings:

**It is Allah Who made the earth a stable home for you and the sky a dome, and formed you, giving you the best of forms, and provided you with good and wholesome things. That is Allah, your Lord. Blessed be Allah, the Lord of all the worlds. (Surah Ghafir: 64)**

Surely, for thinking people every taste is a means to appreciate Allah properly, remember Him with gratitude, to praise Him and give Him thanks. The believer who knows that every delicious type of food and drink comes from Allah; he thinks about this every time he sits down at the table and so he gives thanks to our Lord. Allah says in the Qur'an:

**A Sign for them is the dead land which We bring to life and from which We bring forth grain of which they eat. We place in it gardens of dates**

and grapes, and cause springs to gush out in it, so they may eat its fruits—they did not do it themselves. So will they not be thankful? (Surah Ya Sin: 33-35)

Have they not seen how We created for them, by Our own handiwork, livestock which are under their control? We have made them tame for them and some they ride and some they eat. And they have other uses for them, and milk to drink. So will they not be thankful? (Surah Ya Sin: 71-73)

Some people do not think it is important to reflect on a few extremely important facts even though they have consumed

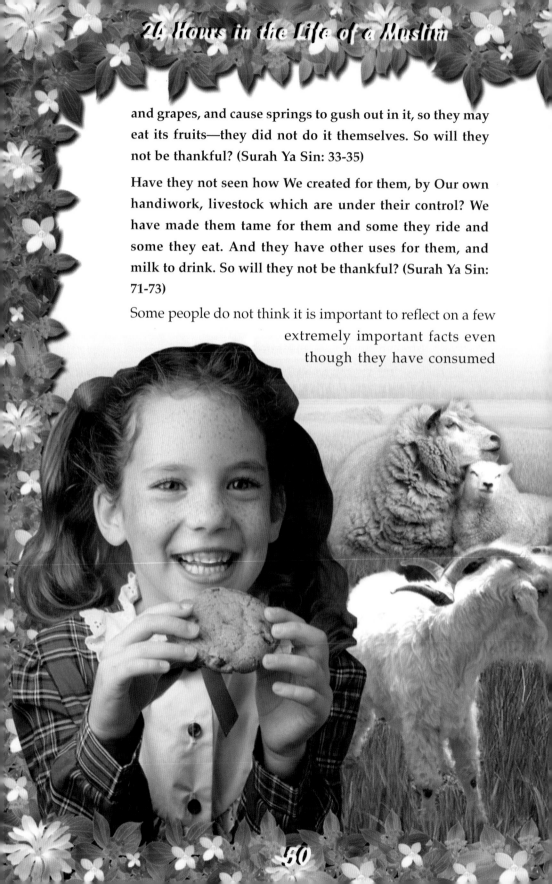

deliciously tasting and smelling foods that have met their needs perfectly throughout their whole lives. They ignore the fact that Allah has created these incomparable blessings for them and that they ought to thank Him for providing them. This is quite the wrong attitude; they should not forget that they will be asked in the afterlife whether or not they had been thankful to Allah.

A believer is aware that Allah has given him his body as a trust, that he is responsible for looking after this incomparable blessing as best as he can and for this he must nourish it in a healthy way. He knows that in order to perform good works it must be healthy and so it must be sufficiently nourished with a balanced diet. He knows his body must have all the food it needs

for the development of its 100 trillion cells and in order for it to renew itself and function properly. So, either for breakfast or at other times of the day he will eat healthy and natural foods and avoid harmful foods no matter how attractive and delicious they appear. He will not be lazy or careless in this regard. For example, he knows that the functioning of his organs, his body's ability to cleanse itself from toxic material and its capacity to overcome fatigue and tiredness all depend on water (which many people neglect to drink regularly) and he will be careful to drink enough of it in the course of the day. Our Prophet, may Allah bless

him and grant him peace, draws attention in several places to the importance of water.

For example, during a trip he sat down somewhere and asked for water from those beside him. After he had washed his hands and face and drunk some water he said to his companions: *"Pour some of its water on your faces and chests."* (Sahih al-Bukhari) Our Prophet, may Allah bless him and grant him peace, said after drinking water:

"All praise is due to Allah Who has made it delicious and sweet by His grace and has not made it either salty or un-savoury." *(Imam Ghazali's Ihya Ulum ad-Din)*

# On the way

People who have finished their breakfast and made themselves ready expect to have various challenges in their work places, schools and other areas. Most people have things they need to accomplish before the end of the day. Allah describes this situation in the Qur'an:

**In the daytime much of your time is taken up by business matters. (Surat al-Muzzammil: 7)**

**… He made the day a time for rising. (Surat al-Furqan: 47)**

A believer sees the day before him as an opportunity to win Allah's love and approval and to attain the Garden for which he needs to strive to do good works. No matter how busy he is, he is careful

never to forget to seek Allah's approval. He takes as his example Sulayman (as)'s prayer, as recounted in the 19th verse of Surat an-Naml, desiring that our Lord will inspire him in the things he will do in the course of the day:

**"My Lord, keep me thankful for the blessing You have bestowed on me and on my parents, and keep me acting rightly, pleasing You, and admit me, by Your mercy, among Your slaves who are right-acting." (Surat an-Naml: 19)**

Everyone who leaves home on the way to school or work encounters many people, things and events to think about. Everything a person sees exists in Allah's knowledge and has come to be by His will and happens for a definite reason. So, when a believer looks up at the heavens with this in mind, he sees that they are marvellously

created. He understands that the truth of the following verse is before his eyes: **"We made the sky a preserved and protected roof ..."**
(Surat al-Anbiya': 32)

The sky's function as a "protected roof" comes from its atmosphere and this atmosphere surrounds the globe and performs its
vital functions so that human beings survive. The atmosphere filters
out rays that come from space and are dangerous for living things; it
vaporises both large and small meteorites that approach the earth
and prevents them from threatening the world and the creatures on
it, and it protects the earth from the freezing

temperatures—approximately minus 270 degrees Celsius—of space. Even if some people do not appreciate this as they should, Allah has created an ideal environment for us and protects us from threats that may come from the heavens.

In the Qur'an, Allah reveals that a believer who observes the heaven will quickly understand the proofs that it is a most harmonious and perfect creation.

**He Who created the seven heavens in layers. You will not find any flaw in the creation of the All-Merciful. Look again—do you see any gaps? Then look again and again. Your sight will return to you dazzled and exhausted! (Surat al-Mulk: 3-4)**

Allah says in the Qur'an that there are signs in the creation of the heavens and the earth for those who observe them with faith.

**Have they not looked at the sky above them: how We structured it and made it beautiful and how there are no fissures in it? And the earth: how We stretched it out and cast firmly embedded mountains onto it and caused luxuriant plants of every kind to grow in it, an instruction and a reminder for every penitent human being. (Surah Qaf: 6-8)**

We made the sky a preserved and
protected roof yet still they turn away
from Our Signs.
(Surat al-Anbiya': 32)

It is He Who created everything on the earth for you and then directed His attention up to heaven and arranged it into seven regular heavens. He has knowledge of all things.
(Surat al-Baqara: 29)

A believer who turns his gaze from the heavens to the earth will see another proof of its creation. Below the earth on which he walks with such confidence there is a layer of unbelievably hot molten rock called "magma". In comparison to this, the earth's crust is very thin, which means that this molten rock is almost under one's feet. So, the thickness of the earth's crust compared with that of the earth itself can be compared to the thickness of apple peel compared with the whole apple. A believer who considers these matters will understand once again that the world and all living things on it exist because of the perfect balance that Allah has created according to His will, and that every creature continues to live in safety and security because of the will of Allah.

A believer who looks with the eye of reflection will notice the beauty around him and the wonders of creation. For example, because they are blessings from Allah, the birds in the sky, the fruits that decorate a grocer's shopwindow with their attractive colours, and the wonderful smell coming from a bakery mean something to a believer that other people cannot grasp.

A believer who ponders the varied and countless proofs he encounters while walking in the street will also be careful about how he behaves. For example, he will walk without exaggeration or display because Allah announces in a verse: **"Be moderate in your tread..."** (Surah Luqman: 19) A humble person obeys the command of Allah and, as in all his other activities, maintains a middle road in the way he walks. This is acceptable both in the sight of Allah and in the eyes of believers.

Believers know that Allah created human beings and endows them with all their characteristics. But those who don't follow the teachings of the Qur'an don't appreciate this fact and think that the qualities they have are their own. These people who think that their beauty, wealth, knowledge and success belong to themselves become proud and arrogant. And because of this arrogance, they want to show their own superiority by crushing others. This attitude is reflected in the way they walk as it is in what they say and do. However, everyone is powerless before the supreme knowledge and power of Allah and we need Allah every moment of our lives. In the Qur'an, Allah warns us about this and forbids us to boast:

**Do not avert your face from people out of haughtiness and do not strut about arrogantly on the earth. Allah does not love anyone who is vain or boastful. (Surah Luqman: 18)**

**Do not strut arrogantly about the earth. You will certainly never split the earth apart nor will you ever rival the mountains in height. (Surat al-Isra': 37)**

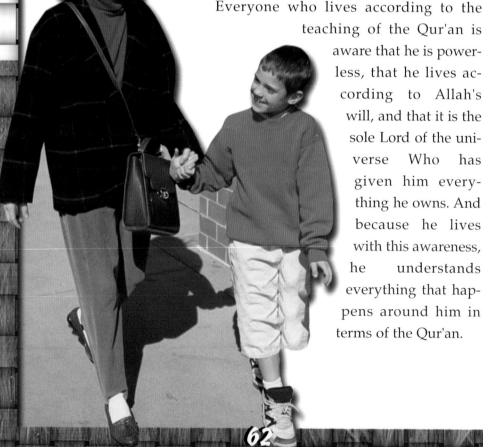

Everyone who lives according to the teaching of the Qur'an is aware that he is powerless, that he lives according to Allah's will, and that it is the sole Lord of the universe Who has given him everything he owns. And because he lives with this awareness, he understands everything that happens around him in terms of the Qur'an.

It is clear that a person cannot cover a lot of distance walking in a day. It is easy to walk short distances, and the ability to walk is a great blessing from Allah. But people can't travel great distances by walking; their bodies becomes tired at some point and they can't walk any farther. Allah knows this weakness of His slaves and has created animals and vehicles to carry them and has made transportation easy. Here are some verses from the Qur'an related to this great blessing of Allah that show His grace, mercy and compassion towards His slaves:

**They (livestock) carry your loads to lands you would never reach except with great difficulty. Your Lord is All-Gentle, Most Merciful. And horses, mules and donkeys both to ride and for**

adornment. And He creates other things you do not know. (Surat an-Nahl: 7-8)

It is He Who created all the species and gave you ships and live-stock for you to ride. (Surat az-Zukhruf: 12)

Do you not see that Allah has made everything on the earth sub-servient to you and the ships running upon the sea by His com-mand? He holds back the heaven, preventing it from falling to the earth—except by His permission. Allah is All-Compassionate to mankind, Most Merciful. (Surat al-Hajj: 65)

By the use of our intellects it is obvious to us that Allah created materials such as iron and steel with certain capabilities and inspired people to use them to make different kinds of vehicles. And it is by Allah's will that people made vehicles such as cars, busses, trains, ships and airplanes. So Allah made it easy for us to go on journeys we could never make by ourselves. What we must do in response to these blessings is to remember Allah when we board these vehicles, praise

His name and give Him thanks. Allah tells us of this in the Qur'an:

**So that you might sit firmly on their backs and remember your Lord's blessing while you are seated on them, saying, "Glory be to Him Who has subjected this to us. We could never have done it by ourselves." (Surat az-Zukhruf: 13)**

Transport today is much faster, easier and more comfortable than it was in the past. For a person who lives according to the teachings of the Qur'an, thinking about this is an important way to draw close to Allah and to thank Him sincerely for His blessings.

A believer also thinks about Allah when he is taking a trip. The person beside him driving the car, the model and colour of the car, the other cars and people around him, their movements, the writing in the back window of the vehicle in front, the row of buildings along the way, their shapes, their windows, billboards and the writing on them are all created by Allah by His decree. Allah announces this to people in the following verse:

**We have created all things in due measure. (Surat al-Qamar: 49)**

Allah created the things we encounter every moment of our lives, not only for a single individual, but also for each of the billions of people on the earth. For someone who lives according to the teaching of the Qur'an, to think about this is a way for him to know that Allah is always at his side, and that He sees his every deed and action. Because the awareness of this fact is with him throughout the day, neither traffic congestion, nor a vehicle swerving in front of him, or any other difficulty he may experience will alter this attitude of submission to Allah.

Some people see even small misfortunes as major adversities; they become impatient and sometimes lose control of themselves, behaving in an irrational way. Heavy traffic or an inattentive driver quickly irritates them and they may start to mutter to themselves or shout. They have no patience when they are stuck in traffic and they show this by continuously honking their horns and irritating others. The reason for such behaviour is that they have forgotten that everything is under Allah's control.

For someone who has turned his back on Allah, transportation is not a blessing but a bother and an annoyance. For example, potholes in the road, traffic congestion, a sudden rainstorm, and many other things will occupy his mind all day. But these useless thoughts are of no benefit to him either in this life or the next. Some people claim that the main thing that prevents them from thinking deeply about these things is the struggle they have in this world. Because of the time they must give to satisfying needs for food, shelter and health, they claim they have no time left to think about the existence of Allah or the signs leading to faith. But this is nothing more than evasion of responsibility. A person's familial duties and the position in which he finds himself have nothing to do with thinking. A person who, in order to win Allah's approval, thinks about the signs leading to faith, Allah's decree, the afterlife, death and reflects on the blessings our Lord

has given him in this life, will find Allah's help at his side. He will see that many of his problems are easily solved and he will be able to find more time and ease to think.

A believer never forgets that Allah has created every situation he meets during his day. The purpose of the creation of these things is for us to learn to be patient or to use our minds to try to solve the problem in the way most pleasing to Allah. If there is a problem that cannot be solved by personal effort, then the only thing to do is to be patient. To become irritated, start shouting and arguing like some people do, is wrong and senseless because it may be dangerous both

for themselves and for others.

It is wrong for people to expect trials to occur only with great pain and tragedy as tests of our patience, because Allah tests human beings throughout the day with various trials both big and small. So, annoying things like being caught in traffic or being late in arriving somewhere and small accidents are tests for human beings. But, in this situation, those who live according to the teaching of the Qur'an do not feel annoyance and they keep their patience without complaining. In the Qur'an, Allah reveals that it is one of the characteristics of believers that they remain patient with the trials to which they are subject:

**Whose hearts quake at the mention of Allah, and who are steadfast in the face of**

all that happens to them, those who establish prayer and give
of what We have provided for them. (Surat al-Hajj: 35)

With regard to traffic accidents that they may have, believers
maintain their composure and are resigned to their destiny, not in a
passive sense, but realistically accepting what Allah has decreed for
them. In such a situation they act sensibly knowing that Allah created what has happened to them and they try to do something to
save the injured, call for help and limit the damage. They know that
they are responsible every moment of this earthly life to act in a
way that will be pleasing to Allah.

In Surat al-Mulk, Allah reveals the purpose for human creation
and the responsibility given to us:

**He Who created
death and life
to test which of
you is best in
action. He is the
Almighty, the
Ever-Forgiving.
(Surat al-Mulk:
2)**

A believer who
lives every moment

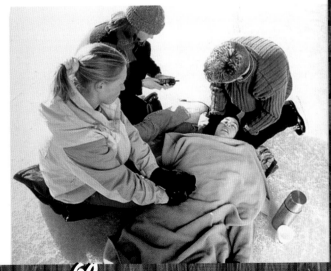

of his earthly life according to the teachings of the Qur'an will not let his mind be occupied by pointless and senseless thoughts during a trip; he directs his attention to things and events about which he can think deeply. For example, those people who are far removed from the teaching of the Qur'an, seeing birds flying through the air, will perceive it as an ordinary occurrence. However, for a believer, the fact that birds, not attached to anything, remain suspended in thin air and per-

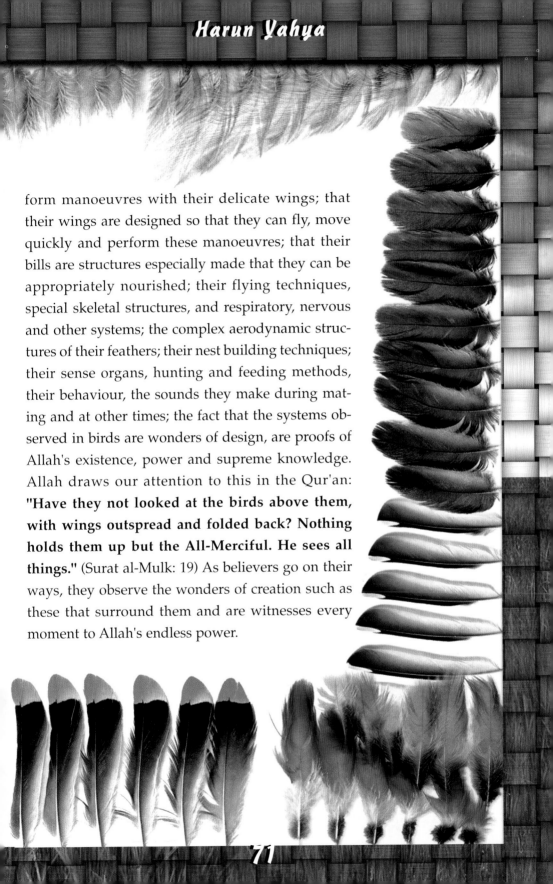

form manoeuvres with their delicate wings; that their wings are designed so that they can fly, move quickly and perform these manoeuvres; that their bills are structures especially made that they can be appropriately nourished; their flying techniques, special skeletal structures, and respiratory, nervous and other systems; the complex aerodynamic structures of their feathers; their nest building techniques; their sense organs, hunting and feeding methods, their behaviour, the sounds they make during mating and at other times; the fact that the systems observed in birds are wonders of design, are proofs of Allah's existence, power and supreme knowledge. Allah draws our attention to this in the Qur'an: **"Have they not looked at the birds above them, with wings outspread and folded back? Nothing holds them up but the All-Merciful. He sees all things."** (Surat al-Mulk: 19) As believers go on their ways, they observe the wonders of creation such as these that surround them and are witnesses every moment to Allah's endless power.

# At work

Most adults devote a large part of their day to work. But those who act according to the teachings of the Qur'an are significantly different from their colleagues, who share a common morality. For a believer, no matter how urgent his business may be during the day, to perform his service to and worship of Allah is more important than anything else. Allah reveals this in the Qur'an:

**...Say: "What is with Allah is better than trade or entertainment. Allah is the Best of Providers." (Surat al-Jumu'a: 11)**

A believer is aware of this, and no work will prevent him from remembering Allah's name or performing his worship; he will not neglect or postpone any religious obligation for the sake of material gain. Our Lord draws our attention to this in a verse of the Qur'an:

**In houses which Allah has permitted to be built and in which His name is remembered, there are men who proclaim His glory morning and evening, not distracted by trade or commerce from the remembrance of Allah and the establishment of prayer and the payment of zakat; fearing a day when all hearts and eyes will be in turmoil. (Surat an-Nur: 36-37)**

The reason for drawing attention to commerce in this verse is because the desire for material profit is one of the biggest weaknesses among human beings. Some people are prepared to neglect the precepts of the deen for the sake of earning more money, obtaining more property or gaining more power. For example, they don't say their prayers or fulfil any other obligations, and they don't display fine qualities of character even though they are able to do so.

There are a number of things that these people expect in return for their labours. They want a good life in this world, to be prosperous, to gain position and respect and be honoured in society, to have a good marriage and praiseworthy children… These are a few of the things that people divorced from the values of the Qur'an even go so far as to choose instead of the afterlife. Indeed, all these things are legitimate blessings to which everyone who aims to win Allah's pleasure and attain the afterlife may also aspire. Believers also want to have the same blessings: useful employment, to earn money and own property. But they have some qualities that separate them from other people: they do all their work to please Allah, spend their money in ways that Allah has advised, and in their business, as in everything else, they meticulously obey Allah's commands.

In a verse of the Qur'an, Allah draws our attention to the dangers of regarding commerce as preferable to the deen:

> **Say: "If your fathers or your sons or your brothers or your wives or your tribe, or any wealth you have acquired, or any business you fear may slump, or any house which pleases you, are dearer to you than Allah and His Messenger and doing jihad in His Way, then wait until Allah brings about His command.**

**Allah does not guide people who are deviators." (Surat at-Tawba: 24)**

A believer with profound faith will make every effort to avoid being caught up in this kind of passion. There is a noble character that Allah expects of believers, and which they will display, no matter in what work they are engaged. In doing business they are honest, sincere, self-sacrificing, hardworking, fair and modest. All their attention is directed to winning Allah's pleasure and to maintaining the boundary He has set between what is lawful and unlawful. Allah has commanded believers that in doing business they should not abuse anyone's rights, they should give full measure and full weight with justice, and not diminish the value of people's goods. (Surah Hud: 85)

In a few verses Allah has revealed the importance of being

honest in business, treating people justly and, in so doing, displaying fine qualities and winning His approval:

> **Give full measure when you measure and weigh with a level balance. That is better and gives the best result. (Surat al-Isra':35)**

> **Give just weight—do not skimp in the balance. (Surat ar-Rahman: 9)**

In the Qur'an, Allah explains how people should engage in trade and commerce. First of all, Allah has clearly forbidden usury: **"But Allah has permitted trade and He has forbidden usury."** (Surat al-Baqara: 275) Another thing that Allah has revealed is how to manage trade and debts. Allah commands that, in doing business, when a person takes on a debt to be repaid after a specified period, he should write it down. If the person incurring the debt is incompetent or weak or unable to dictate, then his guardian should dictate for him justly. And two men among them should act as witnesses. (Surat al-Baqara: 282)

Another thing that believers should be careful about in their work is to consult the views of other people when making decisions, starting a new business, and improving their operations. Allah says in the Qur'an that this is a quality of a believer.

As in every sphere, so in trade and commerce, the Qur'an brings what is finest, easiest and most true into human life. In this way, it helps people away from stress and depression and makes it

possible for them to work in a healthy and peaceful environment where they can submit themselves to Allah, take right action, and consult with others in making decisions.

Besides this, a believer is very open-minded in his work-life making both short and long term plans and mapping out the various stages. And after he has begun the work, he will definitely calculate the further stages, what measures will ensure him success in the long run and possible alternatives. And he will take every precaution that Allah has offered in the Qur'an to ensure that a measure he thinks beneficial to put into effect will not prove disadvantageous at a later stage. While engaged in his work, he will pray constantly to Allah from his heart, ask our Lord to make it easy and he will consider that no enterprise will be successful, unless Allah wills it. He hopes that the work he does will be a way to win Allah's pleasure.

In the age in which we live, new discoveries and scientific de-

velopments have occurred that people in the past could not even have imagined. The teachings of the Qur'an require us to give thanks for these incomparable opportunities. For example, science, technology, modern transportation and communications have reached a high level of advancement today. Thanks to computers and Internet technology, people from all over the world can communicate with one another within seconds, share information and establish contacts. Certainly, these are blessings that need to be pondered very deeply. The prophets Allah has given as examples in the Qur'an always approached Allah sincerely, and always thought about Allah and thanked Him when engaged in their work. In Surah Saba', Allah says:

> **They made for him anything he wished: high arches and statues, huge dishes like cisterns, great built-in cooking vats. "Work, family of Dawud, in thankfulness!" But very few of My slaves are thankful. (Surah Saba': 13)**

# Shopping

Today shopping is an important activity for many people. For example, many people spend hours, even days, visiting stores to find clothes to show off to their friends. They spend a lot of money on clothes that they will wear only a few times in their lives, and despite the fact that their closet is full, they may buy new clothes with undiminished passion. For these people, shopping has gone beyond being a means to meet their needs and become an important part of their lives. It is characteristic of some that they actually lose themselves in shopping and very often buy things that later on they will regret having bought.

Surely, shopping is necessary for everyone and can even be a pleasant chore. But the error in it is that it may instil worldly desires in people and make them completely oblivious of the afterlife. They devote their whole lives, thoughts and plans to this activity, and instead of seeking ways to please Allah Who created them, they try to find satisfaction in minor occupations such as shopping.

As in every area of life, a person who

lives according to the teachings of the Qur'an will also try to see in the activity of shopping the good that Allah has created and the meaning behind things that happen. For him, shopping is not aimless wandering but the opportunity to supply him and his family with what he needs. Shopping will certainly not take him away from performing the service he owes to Allah. Allah commands believers in the Qur'an:

> **Restrain yourself patiently with those who call on their Lord morning and evening, desiring His face. Do not turn your eyes from them, desiring the attractions of this world. And do not obey someone whose heart We have made neglectful of Our remembrance and who follows his own whims and desires and whose life has transgressed all bounds. (Surat al-Kahf: 28)**

A believer who goes shopping will keep the following in mind: Allah has created various foods, clothing and many other blessings for believers. But in many countries, because of unemployment, poverty or conflict, people cannot find anything to eat. Although living in countries with lots of resources, there are people who are too poor to buy what they need. These things are all under Allah's control and there is a reason for the amount of provision that Allah chooses to give people. Allah draws our attention to this in the Qur'an:

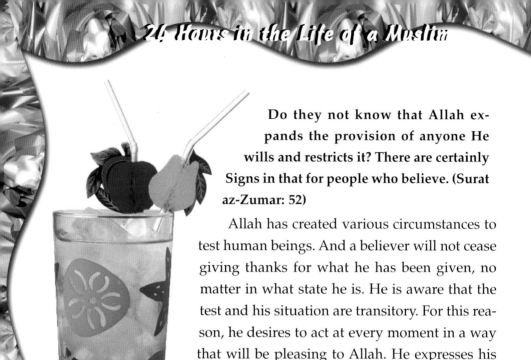

**Do they not know that Allah expands the provision of anyone He wills and restricts it? There are certainly Signs in that for people who believe. (Surat az-Zumar: 52)**

Allah has created various circumstances to test human beings. And a believer will not cease giving thanks for what he has been given, no matter in what state he is. He is aware that the test and his situation are transitory. For this reason, he desires to act at every moment in a way that will be pleasing to Allah. He expresses his thanks to Allah for His blessings in his heart, in what he says and what he does. He spends what he has been given on doing good works, and if Allah restricts his provision, he will be patient and continue to give sincere thanks to Him. He knows he is tested with poverty and prays for Allah to give him patience. In every circumstance, a believer is content with Allah and hopes that Allah will be content with him.

But those who adopt the traditions, customs and values of a society that does not live by the teachings of the Qur'an, immediately lose their sense of gratitude when confronted by the least annoyance. Allah condemns them in the Qur'an, as mut for failing to see that their prosperity and wealth are a trial equal to their experience of poverty and need:

> **As for man, when his Lord tests him by honouring him and favouring him, he says, "My Lord has honoured me!" But then when He tests him by restricting his provision, he says, "My Lord has humiliated me!" (Surat al-Fajr: 15-16)**

Allah has created the countless blessings on this earth, but people who do not realise this forget that it is according to Allah's will and by His permission that they can buy their food and clothing. They do not thank Allah but act constantly under the control of selfish desires. All they think about while shopping is what clothing will most impress their friends. What occupies their minds constantly is where they can buy the latest and most attractive fashions in the colours and qualities they want. They are always concerned about what other people have and are jealous of them. They cannot endure being without possession and material things. They feel a great desire to own property and possessions. They compare what has been given to them with what has been given to others, and become impatient, thinking they have been treated unjustly and do not give thanks. In the Qur'an, Allah reveals the ungratefulness of those who are not content with what they have and always want more:

> **Allah shows favour to mankind but most of them are not thankful. (Surat an-Naml: 73)**

A believer who lives according to the teaching of the Qur'an knows that the blessings around him are a

gift from Allah and is careful not to spend money rashly. While shopping, he makes great effort to avoid wasting money and time. He acts as Allah says in the Qur'an: **"...eat and drink but do not be profligate. He does not love the profligate."** (Surat al-A'raf: 31) He never forgets that Allah calls people who squander their money extravagantly **"brothers of Shaytan"** (Surat al-Isra': 27)

Just as we are required by the Qur'an not to waste money in shopping or buying other things, so generosity is also required. Allah reveals this in Surat al-Furqan: **"Those who, when they spend, are neither extravagant nor mean, but take a stance mid way between the two."** (Surat al-Furqan: 67) This verse sums up the wisdom a believer shows in the way he does his shopping.

# Exercise and physical training

Every person of faith knows that his body has been entrusted to his use for a short time in this earthly life; he is responsible for caring for it as best he can, so he is careful about his health. For this reason, he devotes some serious time in his daily activities for exercise or physical training. Exercise and physical training help to strengthen the body, give it endurance and enable it to function in an orderly and healthy way and will make it possible for the believer to work even better to please Allah and do right action.

A human being's metabolism is not in accord with inactivity, it is created to support movement. Today it is recognised that exercise has many benefits: it strengthens the body's immune, circulatory, respiratory and nervous systems; it makes the body more resistant to germs and disease; it ensures the orderly functioning of the hormonal system, the heart and the arteries; it strengthens the muscles, joints and tendons; in improves conditioning and robustness; it helps maintain balance in the blood sugar, reduce the level of "bad" cholesterol and increase the level of "good" cholesterol.

Another reason why people of faith make efforts in this regard is that physical health is a quality that Allah draws attention to in the Qur'an. For example, it can be seen in verse 144 of Surat al-A'raf, in which Allah speaks to Musa (as) and chooses him to lead the Children of Isra'il, that accounts about him tell of his physical strength. Another verse tells of the physical strength of Talut (as) who was sent to rule over his people:

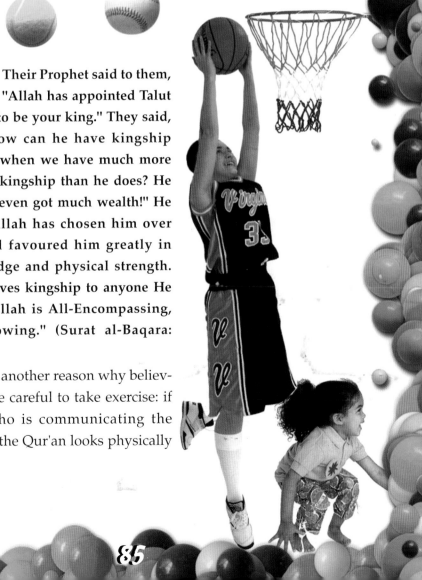

**Their Prophet said to them, "Allah has appointed Talut to be your king." They said, "How can he have kingship over us when we have much more right to kingship than he does? He has not even got much wealth!" He said, "Allah has chosen him over you and favoured him greatly in knowledge and physical strength. Allah gives kingship to anyone He wills. Allah is All-Encompassing, All-Knowing." (Surat al-Baqara: 247)**

There is another reason why believers should be careful to take exercise: if a person who is communicating the teachings of the Qur'an looks physically

strong and attractive he will have influence over others; that person's noble and attractive outward appearance will make a positive impression on those with whom he is communicating.

For this reason, believers should always make the effort to maintain a strong and healthy body. They cannot be lazy, lax or careless in this matter.

# Saying prayers

Verse 56 of Surat adh-Dhariyat which reads **"I only created jinn and man to worship Me"** declares that Allah has created human beings to serve Him. In other words, the purpose of human creation is, as Allah says in the Qur'an, to serve our Lord Who has created all things. So, those who accept the Qur'an as their guide put worshipping Allah above all other things, and they spend their short lives—seventy-odd years if they are granted that much—with a view to the afterlife and to winning Allah's favour. This shows itself in every moment of their earthly lives.

A believer is aware that the teachings of the Qur'an apply not only to a part of his life in this world, or to moments or stages in it, but to the whole life. He obeys Allah's commands to the fullest of his abilities and does as many good works as he can. He spends his time in the acts of worship that Allah has revealed in the Qur'an, and when he finishes one work, he goes on to another. Because Allah says in verse 162 of Surat al-An'am, **"Say: 'My prayer and my rites, my living and my dying, are for Allah alone, the Lord of all the worlds'"**, he pursues what is good and beneficial and there is no break, stop or limit in his efforts. For a believer, beginning a new job after the previous one has been completed is necessary because he knows that he must spend every second given to him in this earthly life working to win Allah's favour, and that he will give account in the afterlife of every moment he has spent in this world. For this reason, he spends every minute hoping only to win Allah's approval, and doing those things that he hopes Allah will most approve of. In the Qur'an, Allah tells believers to exert their efforts in this direction:

> **So when you have finished, work on. (Surat al-Inshirah: 7)**

The believer's actions to win Allah's favour are uninterrupted from one day to another. This is indicated in verse 76 of Surah Maryam: **"In your Lord's sight, right actions which are lasting are better both in reward and end result."**

And in another verse, our Lord reveals that He wants people to persevere in their worship:

> **He is Lord of the heavens and the earth and everything in between them, so worship Him and persevere in His worship. Do you know of any other with His Name? (Surah Maryam: 65)**

The perverse logic of some ignorant people in this regard leads them to doubt the existence of the afterlife and to just perform some acts of worship from time to time.

Some people make the great mistake of trying to get the blessings of this world, which they have set as a goal; they do anything to become rich, gain status and get other things they want. Within a very short time they become engaged in a huge contest for the sake of a **"paltry price"** (Surat at-Tawba: 9) that they will soon lose. But a believer who pursues Allah's favour and the way to the Garden strives only for Allah. The Qur'an describes this quality of a believer:

> **But as for anyone who desires the Hereafter, and strives for it with the striving it deserves, being a believer, the striving of such people will be gratefully acknowledged. (Surat al-Isra': 19)**

A believer who spends his whole day seeking Allah's favour

is resolved and eager in the performance of his prayer. He remembers Allah all day long in his heart and in his activities and ponders deeply His power, intelligence, knowledge, artistry and other attributes. This attitude is the application in daily life of the commands in the following verses:

**… Remember your Lord much and glorify Him in the evening and after dawn. (Surah Al 'Imran: 41)**

**Remember your Lord in yourself humbly and fearfully, without loudness of voice, morning and evening… (Surat al-A'raf: 205)**

In verse 28 of Surat ar-Ra'd, our Lord says that hearts will find peace only in remembering Him:

**…Those who believe and whose hearts find peace in the remembrance of Allah. (Surat ar-Ra'd: 28)**

A person who takes the Qur'an for his guide will be meticulous in performing acts of worship such as praying five times a day, fasting and performing wudu, as Allah has commanded. For example, saying prayers on time is an important matter. He does not let worldly concerns stand in the way of his prayer. Every time he says his prayers, he does it with humility, joy and enthusiasm, hoping that it brings him closer to Allah.

However, those who do not approach Allah with real enthusiasm but for show or out of fear of what other people may think cannot experience joy in worship-

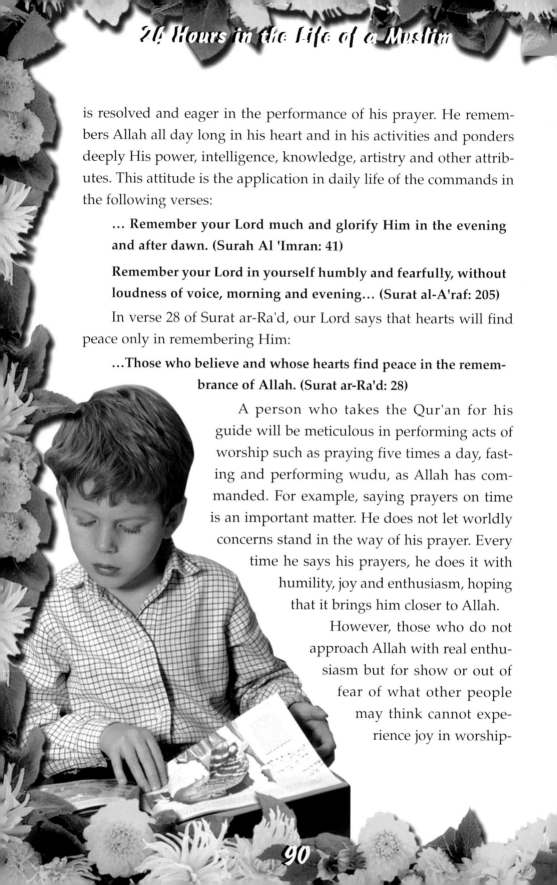

ping Allah. When they perform the prayer, they have no idea that it could bring them closer to Allah. Their minds are too involved in their daily affairs to remember Allah and praise Him. In the Qur'an, Allah gives a warning to those who are neglectful of their prayers:

**So woe to those who do the prayer, and are forgetful of their prayer, those who show off... (Surat al-Ma'un: 4-6)**

This means that they delay the prayer outside of its due time or even don't do it at all. However, although the Surah doesn't refer to it, intelligent people take warning of being distracted in the prayer.

Distracted people make the mistake of thinking that they are doing something for Allah without fearing Him, thinking about Him and without sensing His presence or nearness. The behaviour that will bring a person nearer to Allah consists of sincerity in performing prayers, fear of Allah and obedience and humility before Him.

Some people have a very limited concept of prayer thinking that it is sufficient to obey a few of Allah's commands in the course of the day. But according to the Qur'an, worship is not limited only to religious duties like prayer, fasting, pilgrimage and giving sadaqah.

Worship means service. That is, it consists of a person's attitude and state of mind and everything that he does and says as a slave of

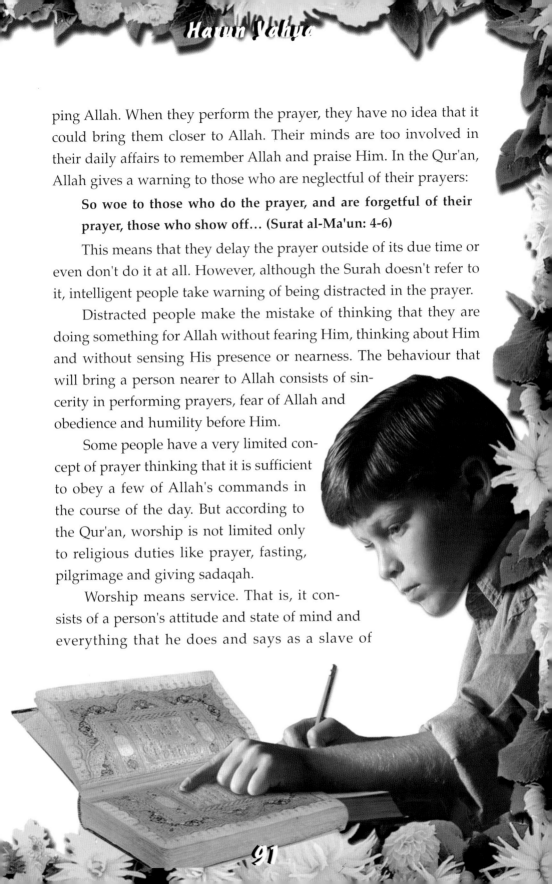

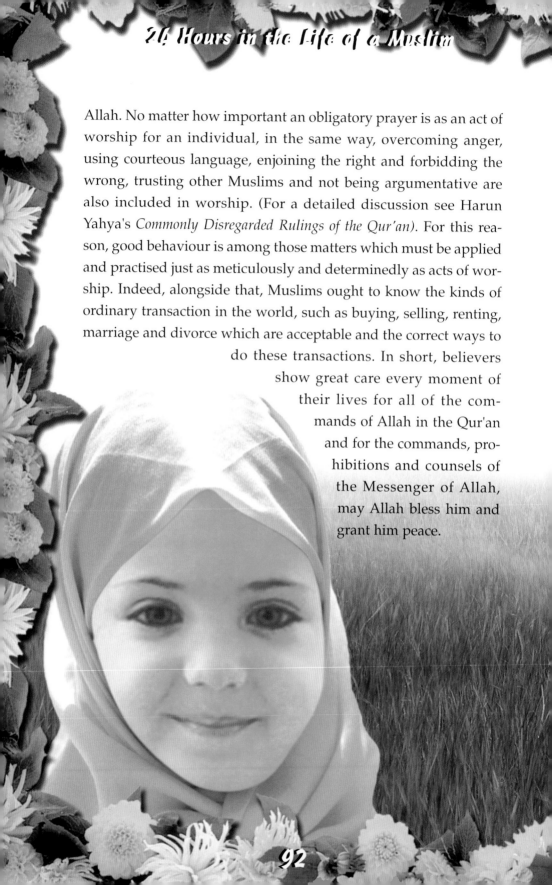

Allah. No matter how important an obligatory prayer is as an act of worship for an individual, in the same way, overcoming anger, using courteous language, enjoining the right and forbidding the wrong, trusting other Muslims and not being argumentative are also included in worship. (For a detailed discussion see Harun Yahya's *Commonly Disregarded Rulings of the Qur'an*). For this reason, good behaviour is among those matters which must be applied and practised just as meticulously and determinedly as acts of worship. Indeed, alongside that, Muslims ought to know the kinds of ordinary transaction in the world, such as buying, selling, renting, marriage and divorce which are acceptable and the correct ways to do these transactions. In short, believers show great care every moment of their lives for all of the commands of Allah in the Qur'an and for the commands, prohibitions and counsels of the Messenger of Allah, may Allah bless him and grant him peace.

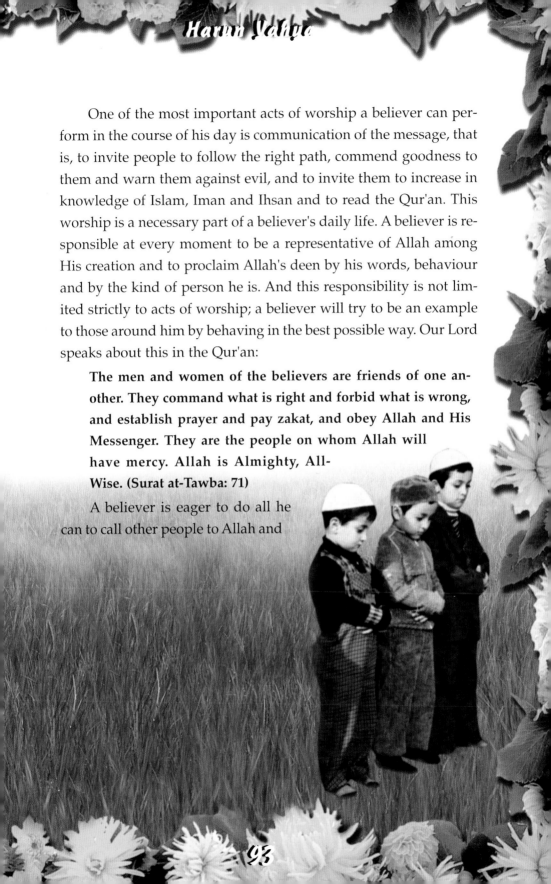

One of the most important acts of worship a believer can perform in the course of his day is communication of the message, that is, to invite people to follow the right path, commend goodness to them and warn them against evil, and to invite them to increase in knowledge of Islam, Iman and Ihsan and to read the Qur'an. This worship is a necessary part of a believer's daily life. A believer is responsible at every moment to be a representative of Allah among His creation and to proclaim Allah's deen by his words, behaviour and by the kind of person he is. And this responsibility is not limited strictly to acts of worship; a believer will try to be an example to those around him by behaving in the best possible way. Our Lord speaks about this in the Qur'an:

> **The men and women of the believers are friends of one another. They command what is right and forbid what is wrong, and establish prayer and pay zakat, and obey Allah and His Messenger. They are the people on whom Allah will have mercy. Allah is Almighty, All-Wise. (Surat at-Tawba: 71)**

A believer is eager to do all he can to call other people to Allah and to His Way. He will tell them about Allah, His Unity and attributes, the purpose of their creation, right behaviour and conduct and the kind of life that pleases Allah, and about good, evil, right and wrong in the Qur'an, the day of judgment, the Fire and the Garden, and other such topics. He will tell them about the Prophet, may Allah bless him and grant him peace, in such a way as to draw them to him, to following and emulating him.

The conversation that believers have among themselves is truly mutual reminder. They call one another to obey the commands of Allah and to live by the Sunnah of His Messenger, may Allah bless him and grant him peace, and to live in conformity with Islamic values. In short, the usual way of a believer is remembrance and reminder.

Believers use both oral and written methods of reminder, and they may make use of today's highly developed means of mass communication. In calling people to the teachings of the Qur'an, they can take advantage of television, radio, books, magazines, newspapers, Internet and other media.

As important as the daily invitation of Islam of believers living according to the teachings of the Qur'an, there is the time they take to prepare the invitation. In the Qur'an, Allah indicates that those who wish to undertake the struggle of ideas on His way must first make preparation for it. For this reason, it is extremely important that a person prepares himself in every way for this work. Allah says:

**If they had really desired to go out, they would have made proper preparations for it… (Surat at-Tawba: 46)**

To communicate Allah's message, one of the things that the believer who is qualified to do so has to do is develop himself and to gain every kind of useful knowledge in order to commu-

nicate Allah's deen. That is, he must educate himself both spiritually and intellectually. He must make every effort to speak and write concisely, to the point and on topic, to be persuasive, effective and to satisfy his listeners with the wisdom learnt from Allah's deen. The main requirement is that a believer learn the deen of Islam, the meanings of the verses of the Qur'an and grasp the conduct and the sayings of our Prophet, may Allah bless him and grant him peace. So, all these preparations and efforts have a special place in the daily life of that believer who is qualified and authorised to call others to Allah and His Messenger.

# Going to bed at night

For all thinking people, there are many matters to reflect on in the creation of the night. Our Lord announced this to human beings in the following verse of the Qur'an: **"A Sign for them is the night: We peel the day away from it and there they are in darkness."** (Surah Ya Sin: 37) One of these matters is hidden in the gradual disappearance of the light and the darkening of the sky. Because of this slow transition, living things easily become accustomed to the differences in light and temperature between day and night and suffer no harm because of them. Allah, with His supreme knowledge and power, has mercy on His slaves and all living things, and He gives this blessing to all people but most do not think of it even once in their lives.

When a person who lives by the values of the Qur'an considers these things, he sees another proof of what Allah revealed in verse 92 of Surah

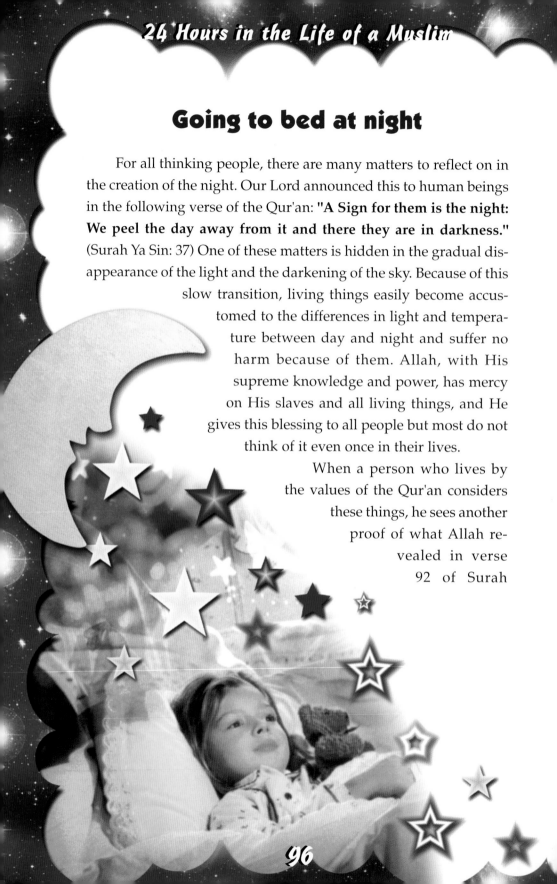

Yusuf: "... He is the Most Merciful of the merciful."

There is no doubt that the alternation of day and night is one of the countless blessings created by Allah for humanity. In order to understand this better, our Lord draws our attention to these things in the Qur'an:

> Say: "What do you think? If Allah made it permanent night for you till the Day of Rising, what god is there other than Allah to bring you light? Do you not then hear?"

> Say: "What do you think? If Allah made it permanent day for you till the Day of Rising, what god is there other than Allah to bring you night to rest in? Do you not then see?"(Surat al-Qasas: 71-72)

Allah created the conditions, balances and systems necessary for day and night, in the absence of one of which, only Allah could help. If Allah wanted, He could create continual day or continual night, but living things could not survive under such conditions. If such conditions ever came about, life on earth would come to an end. There is no doubt that Allah creates day and night in perfect order providing an environment in which living things can survive. This is a sign of His endless compassion and mercy. In the verse following the previous one, our Lord says the following:

> But part of His mercy is that He has made both night and day for you so that you can have your rest and seek His bounty, and so that hopefully you will be thankful. (Surat al-Qasas: 73)

It is only those who use their minds to consider the creation and who come to fear Allah, that is, who live according to the Qur'an, who reflect on the reasons for the orderly alteration of day and night. Allah reveals this in a few verses:

> In the creation of the heavens and the earth, and the alternation of night and day, there are Signs for people with intelligence. (Surah Al 'Imran: 190)

In the alternation of night and day and what Allah has created in the heavens and the earth there are Signs for people who have taqwa. (Surah Yunus: 6)

In the creation of the heavens and earth, and the alternation of the night and day, and the ships which sail the seas to people's benefit, and the water which Allah sends down from the sky by which He brings the earth to life when it was dead and scatters about in it creatures of every kind and the varying direction of the winds, and the clouds subservient between heaven and earth, there are Signs for people who use their intellect. (Surat al-Baqara: 164)

Allah has created human metabolism such that it needs to rest in the night and He reveals this in the following verses:

It is He Who appointed the night for you, so that you could rest in it, and the day for seeing. There are certainly Signs in that for people who listen. (Surah Yunus: 67)

Allah is He Who appointed the night for you so that you might rest in it, and the day for seeing. Allah pours out His favour on mankind but most people do not show thanks. (Surah Ghafir: 61)

Besides being a time for rest, the night has another very special quality. One of the reasons for the creation of night is that these hours of general peace and quiet around the world are productive for some acts of worship. Compared to the active daytime, night-time is more conducive to thinking, reading and praying. Allah reveals this in the Qur'an:

> **Certainly rising at night has a stronger effect and is more conducive to concentration. In the daytime much of your time is taken up by business matters. Remember the Name of your Lord, and devote yourself to Him completely. (Surat al-Muzzammil: 6-8)**

It is easier to concentrate in the night in order to ponder the wonders of Allah's creation, read the Qur'an and pray. A believer who is aware of this will not spend the whole night asleep or resting. He will quietly by himself turn to Allah for his needs, and for forgiveness of his errors and shortcomings. He will evaluate the day that has passed, review the mistakes he made in it; repent of his shortcomings and ask for forgiveness. He will pass his time in a way that pleases Allah, remember Him and try to draw close to Him. He will think about many things such as Allah's existence and majesty, the Qur'an, the extraordinary design of the universe, living things on the earth with their flawless systems, the blessings that Allah continually creates, the Garden, the Fire and eternity. The behaviour of a believer who devote a part of the night to worship is praised by Allah in some verses of the Qur'an:

> **(The slaves of the All-Merciful are) ... those who pass the night prostrating and standing before their Lord. (Surat al-Furqan: 64)**

> **Their sides eschew their beds as they call on their Lord in fear and ardent hope... (Surat as-Sajda: 16)**

What of him who spends the night hours in prayer, prostrating and standing up, mindful of the Hereafter, hoping for the mercy of his Lord? Say: "Are they the same—those who know and those who do not know?" It is only people of intelligence who pay heed. (Surat az-Zumar: 9)

In this way, believers will have put into practice the Sunnah of our Prophet (saas) who spent a part of each night in prayer, contemplation and in worship. This is mentioned in one verse:

Your Lord knows that you stay up nearly two-thirds of the night or half of it, or a third of it and a group of those with you… (Surat al-Muzzammil: 20)

The tradition has been passed down to us that our Prophet, may Allah bless him and grant him peace, prayed that Allah would give him good character and conduct; it is said that he prayed in these words:

"O Allah, make my constitution and conduct good. O Allah, save me from bad character and conduct." (Imam Ghazali's Ihya Ulum-Id-Din)

It must not be forgotten that, as we stated earlier, sleep is like death and, if Allah willed, a person would not wake up again. For this reason, the last minutes before falling asleep may be the last occasion a person has to ask for forgiveness. Allah reveals this in the Qur'an:

Allah takes back people's selves when their death arrives and those who have not yet died, while they are asleep. He keeps hold of those whose death has been decreed and sends the others back for a specified term. There are certainly Signs in that for people who reflect. (Surat az-Zumar: 42)

A believer who lives according to the teachings of the Qur'an knows the value of this opportunity granted to him—perhaps his last—before falling asleep. He keeps this in mind and sincerely draws near to Allah; he asks forgiveness for his wrong actions, asks Allah's help in all things and prays to Him alone in the stillness of the night.

# Chapter 2

## THE QUR'ANIC MINDSET OF A BELIEVER

### Attitude towards family and friends

A believer gives thanks to Allah when he considers the creation of his parents who have spent so much time and labour looking after him over the years since he first opened his eyes to this world. A person who lives according to the Qur'an will always strive to be aware that Allah created his parents and gave them His mercy and compassion and endowed them with love for their children. Allah created a bond of love between parents and the children whom they bring up from helpless infancy until they are self-sufficient adults. In this bond of love, parents never tire of the pleasure of nurturing their children and seeing them grow. Allah stresses the importance of family in human life:

**We have instructed man concerning his parents. Bearing him caused his mother great debility and the period of his weaning was two years: "Give thanks to Me and to your parents. I am your final destination." (Surah Luqman: 14)**

Our Lord says in the Qur'an that we ought to behave well towards our parents:

Say: "Come and I will recite to you what your Lord has made unlawful for you": that you do not associate anything with Him; that you are good to your parents...
(Surat al-An'am: 151)

We have instructed man to be good to his parents ... (Surat al-Ahqaf: 15)

So, according to these verses, a believer will show regard for his parents and treat them with respect, nurture deep love for them, treat them pleasantly and try to win over their hearts with kind and wise words. Again in the Qur'an, Allah shows us how we ought to be sensitive towards our parents:

Your Lord has decreed that you should worship none but Him, and that you should show kindness to your parents. Whether one or both of them reach old age with you, do not say "Ugh!" to them out of irritation and do not be harsh with them but speak to them with gentleness and generosity.
(Surat al-Isra': 23)

In this verse, Allah gives us the measure of mercy to be shown to parents. With the words "do not say 'Ugh!' to them out of irritation and do not be harsh with them but speak to them with gentleness", Allah has forbidden believers from committing the least act of disrespect towards them or neglect of them. For this reason, believers always act attentively towards their parents and with great respect and tolerance.

They will do everything possible to make them comfortable and will try not to be wanting in respect and attention. They will keep in mind the difficulties and anxieties of old age and will make every effort to supply their every need even before they mention it with compassionate understanding. They will do everything in their power to make sure they are comfortable and not in want, either spiritually or materially. And, no matter what happens, they will not stop regarding them with deep respect.

There is another situation that believers may encounter in their relationships with their parents. A person of faith may have parents who have chosen the way of godlessness. In the case of such a difference in faith, a believer will invite them with the same polite and respectful attitude to follow the right path. Ibrahim (as)'s words to his idol-worshipping father show us the kind of approach we should use in such circumstances:

> **Father, knowledge which never reached you has come to me, so follow me and I will guide you to the right path. Father, do not worship Shaytan. Shaytan was disobedient to the All-Merciful. Father, I am afraid that a punishment from the All-Merciful will afflict you, and turn you into a comrade of Shaytan. (Surah Maryam: 43-44)**

Again, when some individuals see their parents growing old and losing their strength, they turn their backs on them when they need help and attention. It is not hard to see that such an attitude is widespread these days. We frequently encounter old people, who are in a very bad situation materially and spiritually, left to live in their houses alone. If we think about this situation we will see that the reason for this problem lies in not living according to the teachings of the Qur'an.

Someone who accepts the Qur'an as his guide acts towards his parents, other family members and everyone around him with mercy and compassion. He will invite his relatives, friends and other acquaintances to live according to the teachings of the Qur'an, because Allah commands those with faith to start telling those close to them about Islam:

**Warn your near relatives. (Surat ash-Shu'ara': 214)**

There is always happiness and joy in a family that lives according to the teachings of the Qur'an as manifest in the Sunnah of the Messenger, may Allah bless him and grant him peace. The kind of shouting, arguments and disrespect we see in some disintegrating families today could never happen in a community of believers. In such a community, everyone takes great pleasure in being with his family. Children treat their parents with respect and love them with all their heart. Families regard children as trusts from Allah and look after them. When we say the word "family", warmth, love, security and mutual support come to mind. But it is useful to point out again that this excellent state can only be reached through living faithfully and completely in Islam and through having fear of and love for Allah.

## Attitude towards blessings

Believers who put aside their habitual views and observe their environment will understand that everything they perceive is a blessing from Allah. They will understand that everything—eyes, ears, body, all the food they eat, the clean air they breathe, houses, goods and property, the things they own and even micro-organisms and stars—have been put at their service. And these blessings are too numerous to count. As our Lord says in the following verse, it is not even possible to classify and count all these blessings:

**If you tried to number Allah's blessings, you could never count them. Allah is Ever-Forgiving, Most Merciful. (Surat an-Nahl: 18)**

A believer can legitimately use all the blessings given to him in this world but he will never be deceived by them and so forget to live without thought for Allah, the afterlife or the teachings of the Qur'an. No matter how many possessions he has, prosperity, money, or power, etc., they will never cause him to become decadent or arrogant; in short, they will never lead him to abandon the teachings of the Qur'an. He is aware that all of these things are blessings from Allah and that if He wills, He can take them back again. He is always aware that the blessings of this world are transitory and limited, that they test him and that they are only reflections of the real blessings of the Garden.

For someone who lives according to the teachings of the Qur'an, the blessings of this world such as property, possessions and position are only means by which to draw near and give thanks to Allah. For this reason, it is never his aim to possess the blessings of this world, which he knows he will only enjoy for a limited time. For example, one of the most enduring blessings of which a person can make use in this life is a house, but it benefits a person for a couple of decades of his life at most. When his life in this world comes to an end, he will go away and leave the house he loved, valued and worked so hard to own throughout his life. There is no doubt that death marks the definite separation between an individual and his earthly blessings.

A believer knows that Allah is the real Owner of the blessings given him and that they come only from Him. He does everything he can to give thanks to our Lord Who created these blessings and to show his appreciation and gratitude. In return for His countless blessings, he will always make every effort to give thanks by what he says

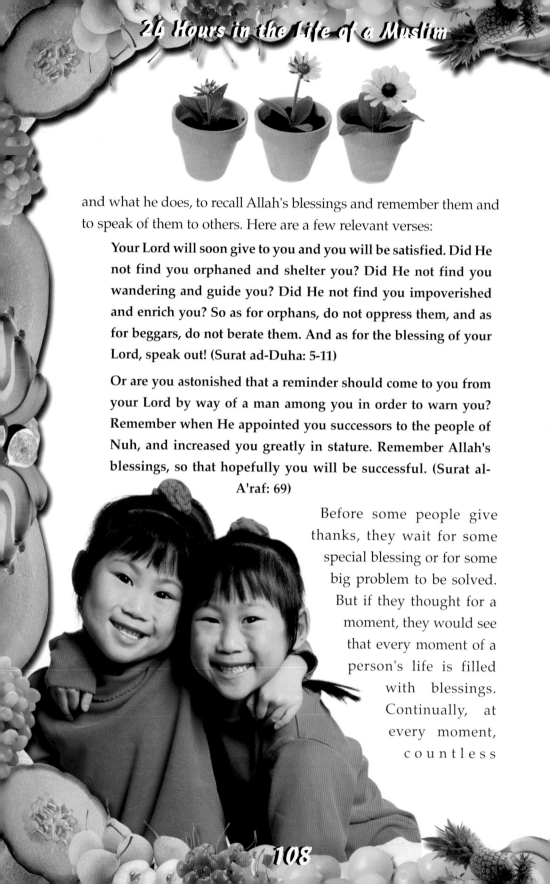

and what he does, to recall Allah's blessings and remember them and to speak of them to others. Here are a few relevant verses:

**Your Lord will soon give to you and you will be satisfied. Did He not find you orphaned and shelter you? Did He not find you wandering and guide you? Did He not find you impoverished and enrich you? So as for orphans, do not oppress them, and as for beggars, do not berate them. And as for the blessing of your Lord, speak out! (Surat ad-Duha: 5-11)**

**Or are you astonished that a reminder should come to you from your Lord by way of a man among you in order to warn you? Remember when He appointed you successors to the people of Nuh, and increased you greatly in stature. Remember Allah's blessings, so that hopefully you will be successful. (Surat al-A'raf: 69)**

Before some people give thanks, they wait for some special blessing or for some big problem to be solved. But if they thought for a moment, they would see that every moment of a person's life is filled with blessings. Continually, at every moment, countless blessings are given to us such as life, health, intelligence, consciousness, the five senses, and the air we breathe. And we should give thanks for every one of these blessings separately. People who are careless in their remembrance of Allah and recollection of the proofs of His creation do not realise the value of their blessings while they have them; they do not give thanks and they only understand the value of these blessings when they are taken from them.

But believers consider how helpless they are and how much they need these blessings, and so they always thank Allah for them. The believers don't only thank Allah for wealth, property and possessions; but knowing that Allah is the Owner of and Ruler over everything, they thank our Lord for their health, good looks, knowledge, intelligence, for their love of their faith and disgust for godlessness, for the fact that they are on the right path, for their association with pure believers, for their understanding, insight and perception, and for their spiritual and physical strength. They immediately give thanks to Allah when they see a beautiful view or when they manage their work well, when they receive something they wanted, hear a good word and witness acts of love and respect, and other such blessings that are too many to mention. They remember Him as the Compassionate and Merciful One.

If a believer shows in his acts of gratitude that the blessings he has received will not make him greedy, arrogant or haughty, Allah will give him even more blessings. This statement of Allah in the Qur'an speaks of this:

**And when your Lord announced: "If you are grateful, I will**

certainly give you increase, but if you are ungrateful, My punishment is severe." (Surah Ibrahim: 7)

At the same time, all blessings are a part of a human being's worldly testing. For this reason, people of faith, in addition to giving thanks, use the blessings given to them as much as possible in doing good works; they don't want to be stingy and hoard wealth. This is because collecting and hoarding wealth is a characteristic of the people of the Fire. Our Lord draws our attention to this in the Qur'an:

But no! It is a Raging Blaze stripping away the limbs and scalp, which calls for all who drew back and turned away, and amassed and hoarded up. Truly man was created headstrong, desperate when bad things happen, begrudging when good things come. (Surat al-Ma'arij: 15-21)

In response to the question as to what people should give away, Allah recommends that one give from **"whatever is surplus to your needs."** (Surat al-Baqara: 219) It is a requirement of the teachings of the Qur'an that believers use a portion of their earnings apart from their own needs for good works as Allah directs. The legal minimum of that is the obligatory zakat, which is collected by the ruler or community leader for distribution to the poor and needy and those others Allah mentions in the ayah about zakat. Giving beyond that is not obligatory but highly recommended.

Certainly believers' thanksgiving for their blessings will be to use the blessings Allah has given them to win His approval. A believer is re-

sponsible for using what he has been given in performing the good works that Allah has commanded. Along with the material means that Allah has given him, a believer uses his body to gain Allah's approval and to work in His way and thereby hopes to win Allah's pleasure and mercy and attain the never-ending blessings of the Garden:

**Allah has bought from the believers their selves and their wealth in return for the Garden... (Surat at-Tawba: 111)**

A community of individuals living according to the teachings of the Qur'an and the Sunnah of the Best of Creation, may Allah bless him and grant him peace, will by their payment of zakat and their voluntary acts of giving remove the violence, strife, theft and other ugly criminal activities caused by poverty, hunger, destitution and other such problems. In this way and Allah willing, peace of mind and well-being will attain their highest level.

## Attitude towards beauty

Because wealth, splendour and beauty are characteristics of the Garden, the imitations of them in this world remind people of the Garden. That increases a believer's eagerness and desire to attain it, but the disbelievers settle for it in this life and show no interest in the afterlife.

Everything—endlessly flowing rivers, places of great scenic beauty, gardens of dazzling colours, human beauty, aesthetic compositions and amaz-

ing works of art—are all blessings and a grace from Allah to humanity. In every one of these blessings in this earthly life there is a hint of the creation of Allah. A believer will regard all beauty in this world as the reflection of an original, and as a model and announcement of good news:

> Give the good news to those who believe and do right actions that they will have Gardens with rivers flowing under them. When they are given fruit there as provision, they will say, "This is what we were given before." But they were only given a simulation of it. They will have there spouses of perfect purity and will remain there timelessly, for ever. (Surat al-Baqara: 25)

However much the blessings in the afterlife resemble those in the world, they are superior to earthly blessings in their reality and in being eternal. Allah has created a perfect Garden endowed with numerous blessings. A person with the values taught by the Qur'an will ponder the creation and excellence of the Garden in everything he sees. When he looks at the sky, he will think of **"a Garden as wide as the heavens and the earth"** (Surah Al 'Imran: 133); when he sees beautiful houses, he will think of **"lofty chambers in the Garden, with rivers flowing under them"**, (Surat al-'Ankabut: 58);

when he sees dazzling jewels, he will think of the adornments of Garden **"gold bracelets and pearls"** (Surah Fatir: 33); when he sees stylish and attractive clothing, he will think of the clothing of the Garden made of **"the finest silk and rich brocade"** (Surat al-Kahf: 31); when he tastes delicious food and drink, he will think of the **"rivers of water which will never spoil and rivers of milk whose taste will never change and rivers of wine, delightful to all who drink it, and rivers of honey of undiluted purity"** (Surah Muhammad: 15) in the Garden; when he sees attractive gardens, he will think of the Garden **"of deep viridian green"** (Surat ar-Rahman: 64); when he sees attractive furniture, he will think of the **"sumptuous woven couches"** (Surat al-Waqi'a:15) in the Garden.

The reason for this way of thinking is that all the beautiful things in the world are for a person of faith the source of great pleasure and occasion for gratitude, whether he possesses any of them of not. At the same time, they are an important source of pleasure that will in-

crease his longing for the Garden and his efforts to attain it.

A believer who lives according to the teachings of the Qur'an will not be jealous or angry when he sees someone who is richer or more attractive than him. For instance, unlike many people he will not regret that he does not have a beautiful house because one of the basic aims in a believer's life is to attain not transient but eternal beauty; his real homeland is the Garden. Allah draws our attention to this in the Qur'an:

> **Their Lord gives them the good news of His mercy and good pleasure and Gardens where they will enjoy everlasting delight. (Surat at-Tawba: 21)**

Those who avoid the teachings of the Qur'an ignore the fact that their real homeland is the Garden and so they are passionately attached to the ephemeral pleasures of this world. Their basic goals are: to be well spoken of, to be respectable and important in their own right, to increase their material means and to live a good life.

Throughout their lives they are constantly running after transient, unimportant and deceptive worldly values. To see good things they do not possess only increases their jealousy, greed and sadness. For example, they take no pleasure in being in a beautiful house that does not belong to them. Their minds are occupied with questions such as these: "Why am I not this rich?" and "Why don't I have a beautiful house like this?" For these people, the beautiful things in this world are usually a source of irritation because in order to take any pleasure from beautiful things, they think they have to own them.

However, those who live according to the teachings of the Qur'an know how to appreciate beautiful things whether they own them or not. For example, a person who has an awareness of his faith may, as a part of his test from Allah in this world, not be living in wealthy neighbourhoods, perhaps not even having seen one. But he realises that there is a definite reason for his situation. A believer knows that he does not have to go to such places to see the beauties of Allah's creation. With his special perception and understanding, a believer will notice the incomparable beauties of Allah's in every place and at every moment. The splendour of the stars at night and the incomparable beauty, colour and design of a rose are two examples that everyone can see and appreciate every day.

As we stated earlier, the longing that believers feel for the Garden causes them to change their surroundings into places that remind them of the Garden. Certainly, the Garden is a place that is a work of art greater than anyone can imagine, with perfect sights and beauties that no one on earth could conceive. But a Muslim who lives according to the teachings of the Qur'an will use all the means at his disposal to beautify his surroundings. We learn from the Qur'an that Sulayman's courtyard was paved with glass (Surat an-Naml: 44) and his house was decorated with high arches and statues, huge dishes like cisterns and great built-in cooking vats. (Surah Saba': 13) In the Qur'an, Allah also says that the family of Ibrahim (as) were given an immense kingdom (Surat an-Nisa': 54).

With the high position, and sometimes great possessions and power that they had been given, Allah's messengers used all their blessings as Allah directed and according to His will. For this reason, they are praised in the Qur'an. Believers take all prophets as examples and take care—as the Awliya (closer friends of Allah) also do—to use every blessing that comes to them to please Allah.

# Reaction to apparently negative happenings

Various difficulties can happen for a person throughout the day. But no matter what difficulties he may encounter, a believer puts himself in Allah's hands and thinks: "Allah tests us in everything we do and think in this earthly life. This is a very important fact that we must never lose sight of. So, when we encounter difficulty in anything we do, or think that things are not going well, we must never forget that our Lord has put this difficulty in our path in order to test our reaction."

In the Qur'an, Allah says that every difficulty a person meets comes from Him:

**Say: "Nothing can happen to us except what Allah has ordained for us. He is Our Master. It is in Allah that the believers should put their trust." (Surat at-Tawba: 51)**

Everything we encounter in our experience is decreed by Allah and is beneficial for the believer in this world and the world to come; this is clear to everyone who observes with faith (For details, see Harun Yahya; *Seeing Good in All,* Islamic Book Service, 2003). For example, there is much benefit when a believer loses some possessions he loved. Outwardly, this appears to be a misfortune but it can be the means whereby a believer may see his mistakes, increase his awareness and realise that he must take much more precaution in some areas. Another beneficial side of this kind of misfortune is that it reminds a person that he does not own anything; that the owner of all things is Allah.

This is valid for every thing, great and small, that happens in the course of daily life. For example, as a result of a misunderstanding or someone's neglect, a payment may be wrongly made; a job on which someone has been struggling with a computer for hours may be lost in one moment as the result of a power failure; a young student may be sick and miss the university entrance examinations for which he spent so much time preparing; due to some bureaucratic transactions, a person may spend days waiting in line; documents may never be completed, thus causing a hitch; a person who has an urgent engagement somewhere may miss his bus or plane…These are the kinds of events that can happen in anyone's life and that appear to be difficult setbacks.

But there is much beauty in these occurrences from the point of view of someone with faith. Above all, a believer bears in mind that Allah tests his conduct and his steadfastness, that he will die and that it is a waste of time for him to dwell on these difficulties since he is going to give an account in the afterlife. He knows there is a silver lining to all things that happen. He never loses heart but prays that Allah will make his job easy and make everything turn out well. And when relief comes after difficulty, he thanks Allah that He has accepted and answered his prayer.

A person who begins his day with this in mind will rarely lose hope no matter what happens or

become anxious, fearful or feel desperate, and if he is momentarily forgetful, he will again remember and turn to Allah. He knows that Allah created these things for a good and beneficial purpose. And he will not think this way only when something serious is about to happen to him, but, as we said before, in everything great or small that happens to him in daily life.

For example, think of a person who does not make the progress he wants in an important undertaking; at the last minute, just when he was about to complete it, he encounters a serious problem. This person bursts out in anger, becomes anxious and miserable and has other kinds of negative reaction. However, someone who believes that there is good in everything will try to find what Allah is showing him by this event. He may think that Allah drew his attention to this in order for him to take more precautions in this matter. He will take every necessary precaution and he will thank Allah that he has probably prevented even greater damage by this action.

If he misses the bus while on his way somewhere, he will think that by being late or not getting on that bus, he may have avoided an accident or other disaster. These are only a few examples. He will think that there may be other hidden reasons such as these. These examples can be multiplied many times in a person's daily life. But the important thing is this: a person's plans may not always turn out the way he wants. He may find himself in a totally different environment than he had planned, but that is beneficial for someone who puts himself in Allah's hands and so he tries to find a divine purpose for everything that happens to him. In the Qur'an, Allah reveals the following:

> ...It may be that you hate something when it is good for you and it may be that you love something when it is bad for you. Allah knows and you do not know. (Surat al-Baqara: 216)

As Allah says, we do not know what is beneficial or harmful; but Allah knows. A person must make friends with and submit to Allah, the Most Merciful and the All-Compassionate.

In this earthly life, a person can lose everything he owns in a moment. He can lose his house in a fire, his investments in an economic crisis or valuable possessions because of an accident. Allah says in the Qur'an that people will undergo this kind of testing:

**We will test you with a certain amount of fear and hunger and loss of wealth and life and crops. But give good news to the steadfast. (Surat al-Baqara: 155)**

Allah tells people that they will undergo various kinds of tests and that they will receive a good reward for their steadfastness in difficult circumstances. For example, a person loses something he owns and cannot find it; the steadfastness that Allah describes in the Qur'an is when a person puts himself completely in Allah's hands and submits to His will from the moment he learns that his possessions, whether large or small, have been lost. He does not lose sight of the fact that Allah has made everything and does not let his attitude or behaviour become unbalanced.

A person may suffer even worse losses in the course of a day. For example if someone loses a source of income on which he spent the greater part of his day in order to meet his needs, that loss is serious for someone who believes that his future depended on it. Many of the people have been brought up from

> I have put my trust in Allah, my Lord and your Lord. There is no creature He does not hold by the forelock. My Lord is on a Straight Path.
> (Surah Hud: 56)

their childhoods with the idea of getting a good job. They spend every moment of their lives wanting a better job or advancement and promotion in the job they have. So, if they lose their job, their days are filled with depression and anxiety and their lives are, as they say, turned upside down.

On the other hand, a believer knows that it is Allah Who gives him his daily sustenance and that his sources of incomes are for this purpose only. In other words, for a believer, the blessings that Allah has given him are only a means. For this reason, if a person of faith loses his source of income, he will accept the fact with steadfastness and submission. In such circumstances, he will be steadfast and pray and put himself in Allah's hands. He never forgets that Allah gives his daily sustenance and that He can take it away anytime He wills.

A person who takes the Qur'an as a guide will immediately take control of his thoughts and actions if he loses a source of income, suffers harm, cannot study in the school of his choice or similar circumstances. He will consider whether of not his behaviour is pleasing to Allah and the following thoughts may go through his mind:

- Was I thankful enough for the goods, property and possessions I lost?

- Was I mean with or ungrateful for the blessings I was given?

- Did I forget Allah and the afterlife in being too attached to my property and possessions?

- Was I haughty or arrogant because of my possessions and did I distance myself from Allah's way and the teachings of the Qur'an?

- Did I try to win the admiration of others instead of seeking Allah's approval, or seek to satisfy my own wishes and desires?

A believer will give an honest and sincere answer to these questions. According to these answers, he will try to correct behaviour that is not pleasing to Allah and pray for Allah to help him do this. He will approach Allah in all sincerity. He will take refuge in Allah from all the wrong things he has done out of forgetfulness or misconduct. In the Qur'an, Allah describes the way those who believe pray:

> ...Our Lord, do not take us to task if we forget or make a mistake! Our Lord, do not place on us a load like the one You placed on those before us! Our Lord, do not place on us a load we have not the strength to bear! And pardon us; and forgive us; and have mercy on us. You are our Master... (Surat al-Baqara: 286)

In being tested, a person can suffer many losses one after the other. But a person with deep faith knows that there is a reason for what he suffers. One of the most important of these reasons is the spiritual training that comes with difficulty:

> ...Allah rewarded you with one distress in return for another so you would not feel grief for what escaped you or what assailed

you. Allah is aware of what you do. (Surah Al 'Imran: 153)

Nothing occurs, either in the earth or in yourselves, without its being in a Book before We make it happen. That is something easy for Allah. That is so that you will not be grieved about the things that pass you by or exult about the things that come to you. Allah does not love any vain or boastful man. (Surat al-Hadid: 22-23)

For a believer, the difficult situations that happen one after another during the day are the means for him to remember that he is in a place of testing to become closer to Allah, to mature and to embrace the teachings of the Qur'an. He is aware that Allah is training him in this way and preparing him for the endless blessings of the life to come.

# Attitude during sickness

A person aware of his faith will be steadfast and put himself in Allah's hands whenever he is sick because he realises that his illness is a test from Allah, just as he realised that his health is a test from Allah. He realises that trials and afflictions are tests from Allah just as are well-being and prosperity and ease, and indeed the latter are probably more serious and difficult tests. For this reason, no matter how uncomfortable he is, he will be steadfast and continue to pray in sincerity to Allah. He knows that it is Allah Who created illness and thus it is Allah Who will give the cure. In the Qur'an, Allah praises the steadfastness of a believer during illness and lists it among the qualities of **"true devoutness"**:

> …**Rather, those with true devoutness are those who believe in Allah and the Last Day, the Angels, the Book and the Prophets, and who, despite their love for it, give away their wealth to their relatives and to orphans and the very poor, and to travellers and beggars and to set slaves free, and who establish prayer and pay zakat; those who honour their contracts when they make them, and are steadfast in poverty and illness and in battle. Those are the people who are true. They are the people who have taqwa.**
> **(Surat al-Baqara: 177)**

While being steadfast, the believer will also take the treatment required to make him better. He will not be emotional or childish to attract the attention of those around him. He will consciously take the treatment and medicine recommended for his illness. This behaviour will actually be a prayer to Allah. At the same time and as a result of living according to the teachings of the Qur'an, he prays constantly that Allah will help and cure him. In the Qur'an, Allah gives Ayyub (as) as an example of this attitude of faith:

> **And Ayyub when he called out to his Lord, "Great harm has afflicted me and You are the Most Merciful of the merciful."**
> **(Surat al-Anbiya': 83)**

It must be said that all medicines taken are means towards a cure. If Allah wills, He will make the treatment a means for healing. It is Allah Who creates the medical means used in treatment—micro-organisms, animal and plant materials—used in the composition of medicines. In short, it is only Allah Who creates the cure. In the Qur'an, Allah draws our attention to this by what Ibrahim (as) says: **"And when I am ill, it is He Who heals me."** (Surat ash-Shu'ara': 80)

However, members of a godless society immediately become re-bellious when they fall ill. They behave in a way quite contrary to the reality of the decree when they say, "Why has such a thing happened to me?" A person who thinks in this way, could never possibly put himself in Allah's hands during an illness or regard it as a benefit.

However, believers think about the reason for their illness and regard it as a good opportunity to draw closer to Allah. Once more they come to understand what a great blessing health is and how helpless human beings are. Even an ordinary sickness like the flu can put a person in bed. In this situation, no matter how powerful, re-spected or wealthy one is, we are helpless and must rest and take our medicine. Under these circumstances, we recall how much we need Allah and our sickness is the means for us to remember Allah's name and draw close to Him. And for the believer, every illness is a warn-ing that the world is transient and death and the next world are close at hand.

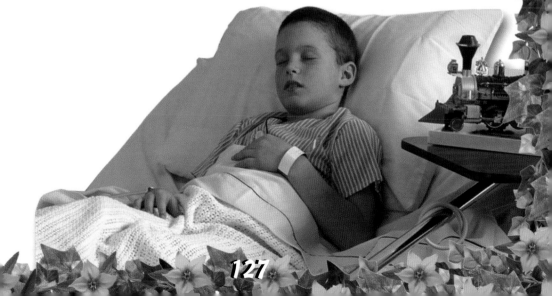

# Attitude displayed in adverse and distressing situations

From time to time, a person may find himself in uncomfortable situations such as on a street corner piled with garbage, in a foul-smelling kitchen or in narrow, dark, dank places. For a believer, even dirty and distressing places have their purpose in creation. These kinds of places remind the believer of Hell and of the misery in that place whose filth surpasses any to be found in this world. In the Qur'an, Allah reveals that the Fire is a place of darkness, dirt and filth:

**"It is indeed an evil lodging and abode." (Surat al-Furqan: 66)**

**And the Companions of the Left: what of the Companions of the Left? Amid searing blasts and scalding water and the murk of thick black smoke, providing no coolness and no pleasure. (Surat al-Waqi'a: 41-44)**

**When they are flung into a narrow place in it, shackled together in chains, they will cry out there for destruction. "Do not cry out today for just one destruction, cry out for many destructions!" (Surat al-Furqan: 13-14)**

A person who remembers these verses will immediately pray that the Lord will deliver him from the pains of the Fire and will ask forgiveness for the things he has done wrong.

According to Allah's description in the Qur'an, the Fire is a foul-smelling, constricted, noisy, dark, sooty, dank smoky place. There are even more dangerous areas within it and a scorching heat that penetrates the cells. The Fire has the most disgusting food and drink.

Garments are made of fire and all its pains are uninterrupted. The Fire is a place where the skin is burnt, a place from which people beg to be released and where they even want to die to avoid the pain, although they have already died and cannot die again. In some respects, the Fire could be compared to the world as depicted in films after a nuclear war. However, the darkness described in these films cannot compare to the extreme filth and depressing environment of the Fire. This is only a comparison and the Fire is much worse and more terrible than the very worst place we could imagine in this world.

Places in this world that are constricted, dirty, dark and hot are very trying for the human spirit. In the Fire, this claustrophobic atmosphere is much worse. Those in this world who had developed methods of protection from the heat will be helpless in the Fire. It is hotter than the hottest desert, more depressing and dirty than the darkest dankest cell. As our Lord indicates in the Qur'an, the heat penetrates into a person's smallest cells. For the wrongdoers there is no protection or relief from the searing heat. Along with this, in the Fire, the senses are much stronger than they are in this world. In this world, most pains grow weaker after a while, wounds heal and even scars from a very serious and painful burn heal with time. A person feels the pangs of the Fire continually and very painfully and this pain never ends, unless Allah wills it to end.

In the following examples we can show another possible reflection on filthy uncared for places: a place may be dirty because of a person's forgetfulness or neglect. However, as soon as the believer sees this filth, he realises just how merciful Allah is towards him and how wrongly he has behaved in return; he recognises that Allah has given him an ideal place in which to live and that he is a guest in that place. Because of this, he realises that he must protect every blessing given to him meticulously and show his thanks to Allah in the work he does. Otherwise, he will be acting in a way that does not earn Allah's approval. A believer who is aware of this will immediately understand where he went wrong and so turn to Allah; he will do the cleaning that has to be done, make up for his mistakes and not fall into the same error again.

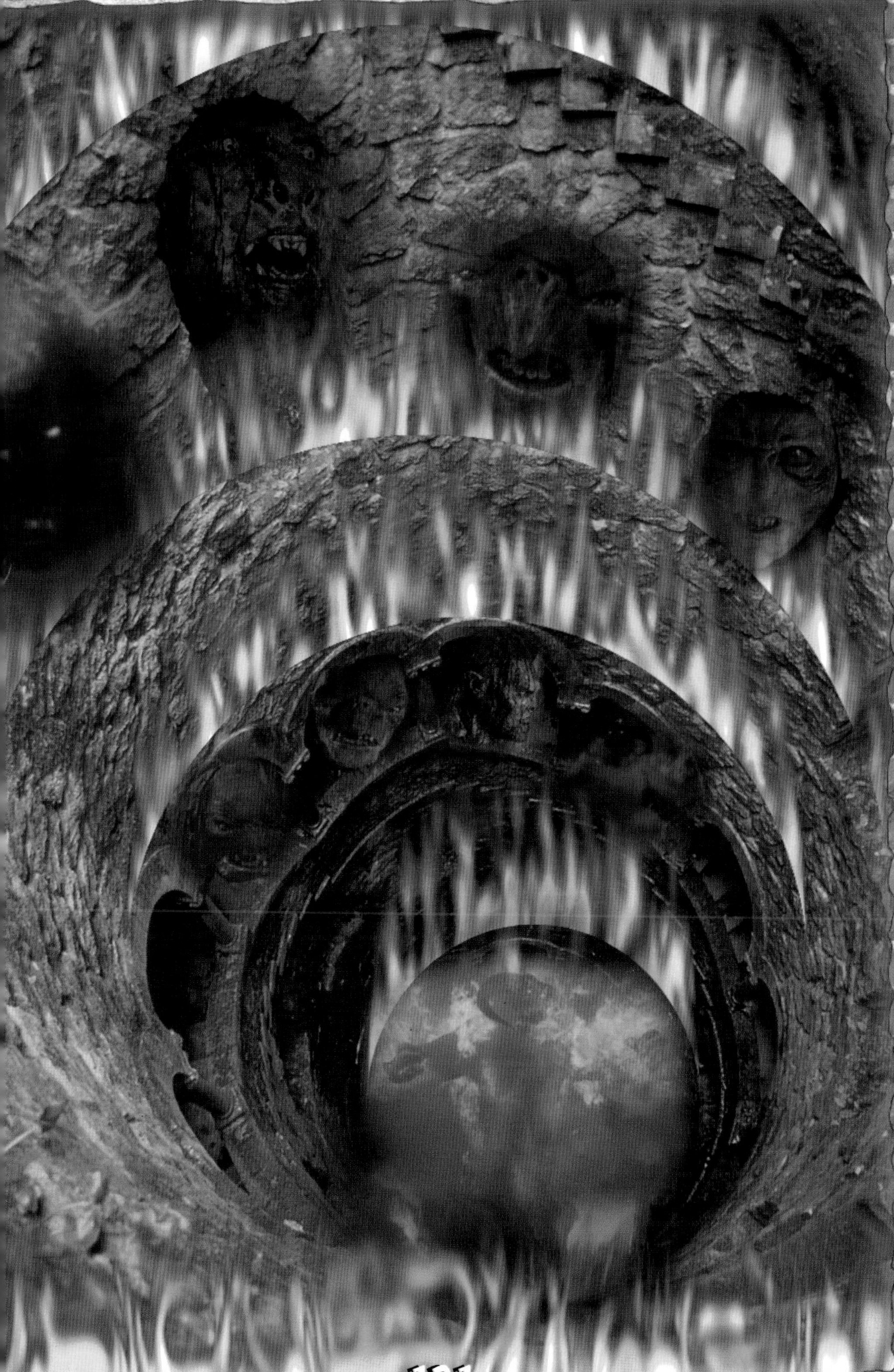

# Chapter 3

## THE SUPERIOR CHARACTER TRAITS OF A BELIEVER

### Vigilance against the wiles of Shaytan

As Allah says in the Qur'an, Shaytan is always trying to divert people from the right path and to take them away from Allah's deen and the teachings of the Qur'an. Shaytan continues his work twenty four hours a day; without making any distinction between rich and poor, young and old, pretty or unattractive, and he expends much effort trying to mislead everyone. He feels resentment towards everyone no matter who they are.

Shaytan was filled with this resentment at the creation of the first human being. After Allah created Adam, He ordered Shaytan to prostrate to him but Shaytan was filled with pride and jealousy; he disobeyed Allah and refused to prostrate. As a result of this rebellion and insolence he was driven from the presence of Allah. Our Lord tells us about this in the Qur'an:

**We created you and then formed you and then We said to the angels, "Prostrate before Adam," and they prostrated—except for Iblis. He was not among those who prostrated. He (Allah)**

said, "What prevented you from prostrating when I commanded you to?" He (Iblis) replied, "I am better than him. You created me from fire and You created him from clay."

He (Allah) said, "Descend from Heaven. It is not for you to be arrogant in it. So get out! You are one of the abased." (Surat al-A'raf: 11-13)

Allah tells us in the Qur'an that Shaytan blamed human beings for his fallen condition and asked Allah for a period of time—ending at the Day of Judgment—in which he would begin his work of tempting man from the right path.

He said, "Grant me a reprieve until the day they are raised up."

He (Allah) said, "You are one of the reprieved."

He said, "By Your misguidance of me, I will lie in ambush for them on Your straight path. Then I will come at them, from in front of them and behind them, from their right and from their left. You will not find most of them thankful."

He (Allah) said, "Get out of it, reviled and driven out. As for those of them who follow you, I will fill up Hell with every one of you." (Surat al-A'raf: 14-18)

Shaytan's target is all humanity beginning with believers who strongly embrace Allah's religion. His desire is to draw as many people as possible to be with him in the Fire. He tries to prevent people from worshipping Allah sincerely from the heart, to take people away from Allah's deen and from the Qur'an and, as a result, to draw them into endless punishment.

And those with faith are aware that their greatest enemy, Shaytan, is always working; while they are trying to obey the commands of Allah as best they can, they are always wary of Shaytan's games and tricks. They are awake to the apprehension and groundless fears that he causes and his incitements to act against the teachings of the Qur'an or to put it aside and forget it and to part from the way of Allah. An example of the insinuations Shaytan puts in the mind of man is found in verse 268 of Surat al-Baqara:

**Shaytan promises you poverty and commands you to avarice. Allah promises you forgiveness from Him and abundance. Allah is All-Encompassing, All-Knowing. (Surat al-Baqara: 268)**

As this verse says, Shaytan tries to get a person who has lost his job to forget that Allah gives sustenance to every human being, and makes him afraid that he will not be able to find any money and so will go hungry. By instilling this kind of fear and by making other kinds of insinuations, he tries to draw people to his side. In the Qur'an, Allah shows human beings what to do against the evil impulses Shaytan provokes in us.

**If an evil impulse from Shaytan provokes you, seek refuge in Allah. He is All-Hearing, All-Seeing. As for those who have taqwa, when they are bothered by visitors from Shaytan, they remember and immediately see clearly. (Surat al-A'raf: 200-201)**

The most important thing a person can do to protect himself against the wiles of Shaytan is to take refuge with Allah. He must not forget that Shaytan is also under Allah's control and does not have the power to do anything unless Allah wills it. In the Qur'an,

Allah commands us to say this prayer in order to take refuge with Him from Shaytan:

> Say: "I seek refuge with the Lord of mankind, the King of mankind, the God of mankind, from the evil of the insidious whisperer who whispers in people's breasts and comes from the jinn and from mankind." (Surat an-Nas: 1-6)

A person who possesses the qualities taught in the Qur'an will always take refuge with Allah from Shaytan and will know the difference between the insinuations of Shaytan that pass through his mind, as if his own thoughts, and thoughts which conform to the Qur'an. He will be alert at every moment and pay no attention to what Shaytan says. He will not let Shaytan interfere in anything he thinks or does. For example, whether busy with his work, or alone by himself, or speaking with someone, when something happens to him or when some difficulty occurs, he always acts with the awareness that Shaytan is waiting in ambush tempting him to speak and act in a way not pleasing to Allah. In this and every situation he will speak and act in a way that conforms to the Qur'an. In this way believer will not fall under the influence of the wiles of Shaytan. Our Lord tells us about this in the Qur'an:

> He (Shaytan) has no authority over those who believe and put their trust in their Lord. He only has authority over those who take him as a friend and associate others with Allah. (Surat an-Nahl: 99-100)

# Understanding, tolerance and forgiveness

According to Allah's command, "... **Be good to your parents and relatives and to orphans and the very poor, and to neighbours who are related to you and neighbours who are not related to you, and to companions and travellers and your slaves**" in verse 36 of Surat an-Nisa', believers behave well towards those around them. They are never quarrelsome, contrary or negative but interact with people positively and correctly. Because they live according to the teachings of the Qur'an, they display a character that is conciliatory and open to communication. They know that the anger, quarrelsomeness and argumentativeness of those who live without the deen have no place in the way taught by the Qur'an. For this reason, they are forgiving, tolerant and try to see the good in the other. In the Qur'an, Allah draws our attention to this as an expression of a superior character:

> **But if someone is steadfast and forgives, that is the most resolute course to follow. (Surat ash-Shura: 43)**

Allah commands us to be understanding, tolerant and forgiving toward others. He commands this in the following verse:

> **Those of you possessing affluence and ample wealth should not make oaths that they will not give to their relatives and the very poor and those who have emigrated in the way of Allah. They should rather pardon and overlook. Would you not love Allah to forgive you? Allah is Ever-Forgiving, Most Merciful. (Surat an-Nur: 22)**

For this reason, a believer is careful to treat any believer he has to deal with in his daily life with understanding and tolerance. For example, he will be understanding towards a believer who makes noise and wakes him up in the morning. He knows that he acts only by Allah's decree; Allah wanted him to wake up at that moment and the person making the noise was His instrument. This is one possible way of seeing it. However, this would be an occasion for some people to become irritated and quarrelsome. A believer is careful to behave politely to other believers who harm him by accident. No matter how serious the situation, he does not become angry, lose his composure or upset those around him. He hopes for the same kind of understanding from others when he himself makes a mistake. As we said earlier, he hopes that Allah in His infinite mercy will forgive him his wrong actions. If he does not attempt to exemplify Allah's attribute as the "Ever-Forgiving" in his own behaviour, he knows that this attitude will lead him to act contrary to the teachings of the Qur'an.

A person who lives according to the teachings of the Qur'an will have fine qualities of character. Because of the maturity he shows in the course of the day at home, at school or at work, he prevents any tension or anxiety from arising. Moreover, the behaviour of a believer will be an example to others. The most important thing is that his behaviour is that which is praised in the Qur'an and he acts in a way that is pleasing to Allah.

From the information he collected from scholars, Imam al-Ghazali wrote the following about the exemplary behaviour of our Prophet, may Allah bless him and grant him peace, towards those around him:

"... He used to be the first to greet one whom he met. He did not stand up or sit down without remembering Allah...

... He used to call his companions by their honorifics to honour them and he used to give honorifics to those who had none.

... He was very affectionate and kind in dealing with people." *(Imam al-Ghazzali's Ihya Ulum-Id-Din)*

Surely what we have to emulate is the noble character of our Prophet, may Allah bless him and grant him peace. Those who adopt the values of the Qur'an and follow the Sunnah of our Prophet, may Allah bless him and grant him peace, can hope to live a good life in this world by Allah's will and receive a great blessing from Allah in the Hereafter.

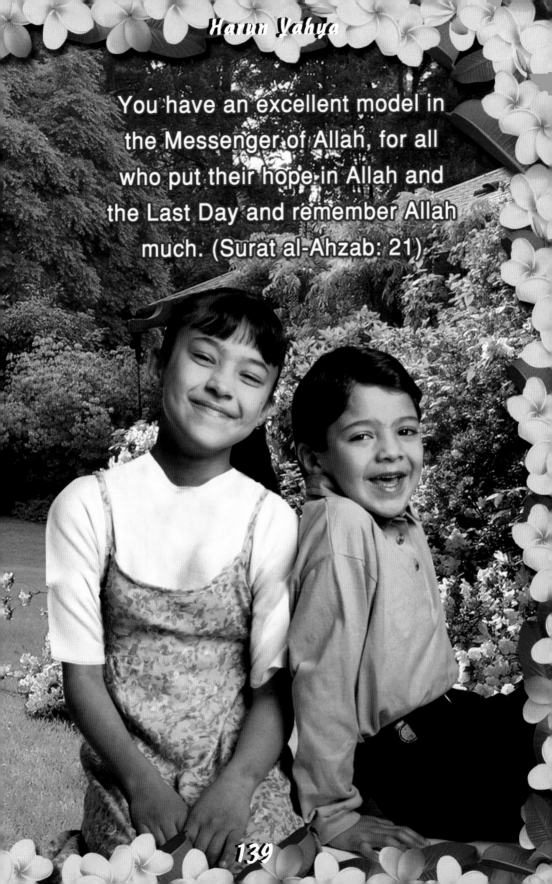

You have an excellent model in the Messenger of Allah, for all who put their hope in Allah and the Last Day and remember Allah much. (Surat al-Ahzab: 21)

# Steadfastness

In almost every society there are people, who are not believers but who live more or less according to the values that Allah has described in the Qur'an. When it is necessary, these people can behave helpfully, gently and with self-sacrifice, mercy and justice. But no matter how much these people claim to have good moral qualities, they will certainly have their moments when they will not steadfastly maintain this behaviour. For example, someone who has to take an important examination may oversleep in the morning because his watch is broken. When he wakes up he hurries to school and gets caught in dense traffic. He wants to telephone the school to let them know he will be late but all the lines are busy. If a friend sitting beside him asks him a question at this point, he may answer with a peevish tone of voice, or just look at him crossly without giving an answer. This person thinks himself a helpful and understanding person, but in a situation like this we might say his patience has run out and he behaves in an unhelpful way.

In every situation and in all circumstances, a believer is determined to act by the values of the Qur'an in the way he lives. He is patient with others who say and do things that are wrong or unpleasant. (For a detailed discussion see Harun Yahya's *The Importance of Patience in the Qur'an*)

For example, someone pushes him out of the way in order to get on the bus first. A friend might say harsh things to him in anger. A careless driver of a passing car might cover him with mud from head to toe as he walks along the road. The possible examples could be multiplied. But a person who has espoused the teachings of the Qur'an will realise that all these things are created this way in his destiny and will never behave in an unseemly, irritated or peevish way. Of course, he will take every precaution against such a thing happening again, and will do everything he can to avoid things that cause irritation. According to the values taught in the Qur'an, even in the case when something happens that causes one harm, a person must be patient with others and if possible repay bad behaviour shown him with better. In the Qur'an, Allah draws our attention to the fact that, through their patience, believers can repel bad actions kindly:

> **A good action and a bad action are not the same. Repel the bad with something better and, if there is enmity between you and someone else, he will be like a bosom friend. None will obtain it but those who are truly steadfast. None will obtain it but those who have great good fortune. (Surah Fussilat: 34-35)**

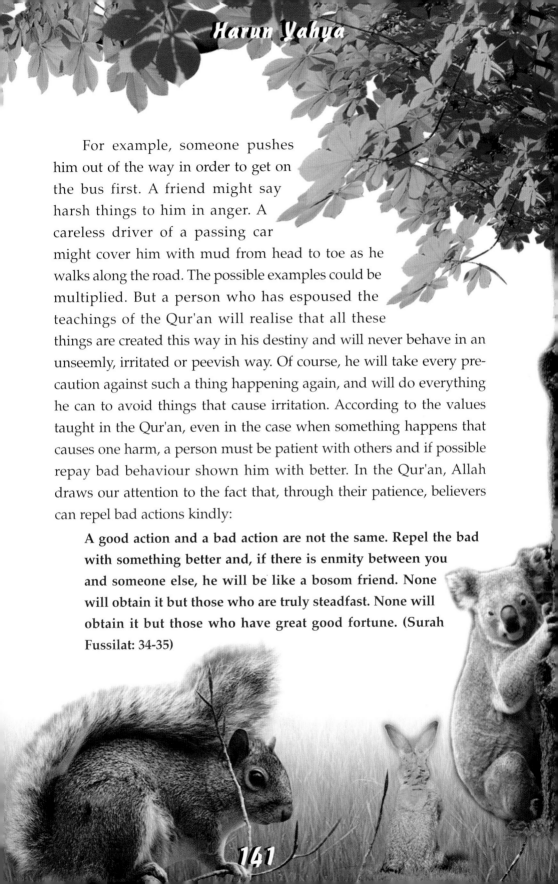

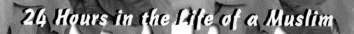

## Good words

Some people, even if their consciences tell them to be forgiving towards someone who has wronged them or to speak politely to someone who has spoken harshly to them, prefer not to forgive and to answer the insult with a greater one. According to this warped way of thinking, to speak peevishly, to ridicule another person with arrogant and insulting words and to respond with insolence and disrespect is actually a sign of superiority.

Of course, these ideas are totally contrary to the Qur'an. In the Qur'an, Allah gives us the following examples of how blessed polite language is and how it always brings benefit to human beings:

**Do you do not see how Allah makes a metaphor of a good word: a good tree whose roots are firm and whose branches are in heaven? It bears fruit regularly by its Lord's permission. Allah makes metaphors for people so that hopefully they will pay heed. The metaphor of a corrupt word is that of a rotten tree, uprooted on the surface of the earth. It has no staying-power. Allah makes those who believe firm with the Firm**

**Word in the life of this world and the Hereafter. But Allah misguides the wrongdoers. Allah does whatever He wills. (Surah Ibrahim: 24-27)**

As we see in this verse, a person who speaks edifying words and lives according to them will find great beauty and incomparable blessings both in this world and in the world to come. On the other hand, a person who speaks unedifying words and lives according to them is walking along a dark road that will end in the Fire.

A believer speaks well and wisely to everyone he meets during the day. Wherever he may be, he speaks about Allah's deen, gives advice from the Qur'an, speaks words that recall Allah and the good character of the Messenger of Allah, may Allah bless him and grant him peace, and speaks to people with respect. In order to encourage his friends, he praises their good qualities that correspond

to the teachings of the Qur'an and the Sunnah and he speaks in a way that will help people to continue through the day more joyfully and lively. We may compare this behaviour of believers to the good fruit tree in the verse above.

However, some people prefer not to speak about the good qualities of others but want to humiliate them by pointing out their errors and shortcomings. As we pointed out, in the verses in Surah Ibrahim, our Lord draws our attention to this and compares this kind of language to a corrupt tree that bears no fruit. Just as a harsh word destroys a good relationship, it will also dampen the enthusiasm of the other party and be the cause of sorrow and regret.

On the other hand, when a believer speaks with someone giving him advice about how to remedy his shortcomings or pointing out his errors, he will take care to choose the best words. In doing this he will be fulfilling the following command of Allah:

**Say to My slaves that they should only say the best. Shaytan wants to stir up trouble between them. Shaytan is an outright enemy to man. (Surat al-Isra': 53)**

As Allah says in this verse, Shaytan tries to get people not to say good things to one another and, in this way, to make them enemies. When a negative word is spoken, Shaytan immediately starts to introduce suspicions to pry each side apart. A person who feels uncomfortable because he has been addressed unpleasantly will be

influenced by the insinuations of Shaytan and respond in the same way to his opponent. This will damage or even destroy their friendship. But a positive word will avert the possibility of Shaytan's drawing people into error. For this reason, believers make every effort to speak to one another as positively as possible so that Shaytan will not have the occasion or the conditions to interfere. Such an attitude will be the means by which they will increase their bond of friendship. Our Prophet, may Allah bless him and grant him peace, has commanded believers always to practice high conduct and to speak positively:

> "Do not envy one another; do not hate one another; do not turn away from another; and do not undercut one another, but be you, O slaves of Allah, brothers." *(Muslim)*

> "Greeting a person is charity. Acting justly is charity. A good word is charity." *(Bukhari and Muslim)*

> "There is nothing heavier in the scales than good character." *(Imam Ahmad and Abu Dawud)*

# Thoughtfulness

In a society in which the values of the Qur'an are not dominant, there are people who are crude, impolite, thoughtless and disrespectful. But believers carefully avoid these kinds of manners and behaviour; they have a quality of character that is irreproachable, polite, sensitive and thoughtful. These are also qualities of Allah's Messengers. In the Qur'an we are told about Musa (as)'s subtle way of thinking:

> When he arrived at the water of Madyan, he found a crowd of people drawing water there. Standing apart from them, he found two women, holding back their sheep. He said, "What are you two doing here?" They said, "We cannot draw water until the shepherds have driven off their sheep. You see our father is a very old man." So he drew water for them and then withdrew into the shade and said, "My Lord, I am truly in need of any good You have in store for me." (Surat al-Qasas: 23-24)

Being a sensitive man, Musa (as) immediately recognised that the women he met were in need and he helped them without wasting any time. This characteristic of Musa (as) is praised in the Qur'an and people of faith take it as an example in their daily lives. When they see someone who is in a difficult or anxious state they immediately try to do everything they can to help. Besides this, they try to cheer them up and in order to create a happy and beautiful ambiance, they act nobly in a way that will please them.

It is a quality of thoughtfulness to act in a way that will not make people uncomfortable. A person in a family situation who keeps shared things and areas clean and in order, avoids speaking loudly or listening to music loudly where he may make someone uncomfortable, observes whether or not the person he wants to talk to is free to listen to him at that moment, and doesn't hinder someone who is in a hurry trying to do something, is an example of the thoughtfulness that we often encounter in daily life.

Another important indication of thoughtfulness is recognising the precedence of others. In a conversation in which two people are talking on something about which they both know and one of them lets the other speak and someone who lets someone else take the last bit of food are examples of this. Apart from that, offering your seat on a bus to someone who needs it, and letting someone go ahead of you at the check-out after you have finished your shopping are ways in which people can get close to each other and establish good relations. People who are thoughtful towards others will establish sound relationships based on love and respect. In addition, they will enjoy living with the people in their neighbourhood and take pleasure in seeing them again.

On the other hand, in an environment where everyone is trying to do things for others for the advantage and profit they can get out of it, true friendship cannot exist. Putting on airs in conversation and artificial behaviour prevents friendship from forming. Empty chat and sarcasm create a tense atmosphere and no one would want to be in such places where there is no thought for Allah.

# Hospitality

In the verses where Ibrahim (as)'s care for his guests is described, the Qur'an shows how to be a host according to the teachings of the Qur'an:

**Has the story reached you of the honoured guests of Ibrahim?**

**When they entered his dwelling and said, "Peace!" he said, "Peace, to people we do not know."**

**So he slipped off to his household and brought a fattened calf.**

**He offered it to them and then exclaimed, "Do you not then eat?" (Surat adh-Dhariyat: 24-27)**

Believers who take Ibrahim (as)'s hospitality as an example will greet their guests cheerfully with a warm welcome and make them comfortable by showing them respect and love. Then, they will think about what their guests may need, and supply it without their having to say or intimate anything. Moreover, they will try to offer these things without delay because it is the custom of the Muslims based on the personal example of the Messenger of Allah, may Allah bless him and grant him peace, that guests must be offered the best food in the house.

However, some individuals do not open the door when guests come calling even if they know them, and are forced against their will to entertain guests. They receive them out of custom or social necessity. Their behaviour changes according to the status of their guest: when hosting a poor person, they try to make do without offering special treats. But if their guest is rich and influential, they go beyond offering small treats and make every effort to offer the best possible food with the best possible service.

When a host treats his guests coldly and with disregard for their feelings, certainly he makes them uncomfortable and they feel uneasy. This makes for a situation that each side wants to end soon. The guest is sorry for having come, and the host is sorry for having provided the food and wasted his time.

In conclusion, it is only by practicing the teachings of the Qur'an and emulating the noble and generous behaviour of the last Messenger, may Allah bless him and grant him peace, and the behaviour of the right-acting Muslims right down to our own day that fine conversation and hospitality, unity and cooperation can grow among people.

# Mutual peace and respect

When believers meet during the day, they offer one another their heartfelt best wishes; in other words, they wish each other peace. By doing this, they fulfil Allah's recommendation: **"When you are greeted with a greeting, return the greeting or improve on it..."** (Surat an-Nisa': 86) In another verse, Allah advises believers to offer the greeting of peace when they enter houses:

> **...And when you enter houses greet one another with a greeting from Allah, blessed and good. In this way Allah makes the Signs clear to you so that hopefully you will use your intellect. (Surat an-Nur: 61)**

When a believer leaves his house, he pleasantly wishes the neighbours he meets a good day and Allah's peace and mercy. He greets people on the street, his friends at school and other people in the same way. If someone greets him, no matter who, he receives his greeting and gives him an even better one in return. This behaviour is one of the beautiful things brought by the Qur'an and Sunnah to social relationships. By offering a greeting of peace, the cold and tense atmosphere between people who do not know one another is removed. People come closer together and a warm atmosphere is created among them even if they don't know one another.

In ordinary society, however, the greeting of peace is generally done out of habit. Some people greet only those from whom they make, or hope to make, some profit. Sometimes they do not receive the greeting from people they regard as inferior in status to themselves, or pretend not to hear it, in order to humiliate them. More seriously, such behaviour is regarded as normal in some circles.

Allah calls to the Abode of Peace and He guides whom He wills to a straight path. Those who do good will have the best and more! Neither dust nor debasement will darken their faces. They are the Companions of the Garden, remaining in it timelessly, for ever. (Surah Yusuf: 25-26)

# Avoiding anger and dispute

Disputes are cause for people falling out with each other, becoming at variance, fight and conflicts. If a small argument between two friends grows, anger can replace all their positive feelings. In verse 54 of Surat al-Kahf, Allah draws our attention to this negative quality, and says that human beings are, above all, argumentative. For this reason, believers must at all costs avoid every kind of argument that may weaken or destroy their spirit of unity, togetherness and brotherhood. Allah clearly forbids this kind of behaviour:

**Obey Allah and His Messenger and do not quarrel among yourselves lest you lose heart and your momentum disappear...
(Surat al-Anfal: 46)**

Quarrels break believers' strength, offer no solution to a problem, are of no benefit and come about at the instigation of Shaytan. If a person in good conscience regards arguments and fights as ugly and unacceptable, even so his lower self may push him towards dispute and conflict. For this reason, someone who takes the Qur'an as his guide and always acts according to his conscience will never allow argumentativeness to develop. Even if an argument breaks out as a result of some moment of carelessness, he will collect himself, remember Allah's command, realise that what he did was not pleasing to Allah and abandon this kind of behaviour.

A person with faith may meet various kinds of people throughout the day but will at all costs avoid argument. For example, while doing his shopping he will not engage in argument with the shopowner over prices, or with a bus driver because the bus is late, or with a slow official while waiting in a queue. If he is in a situation where he is treated unfairly, he will not become angry and start an argument but will choose to resolve the situation by acting positively and intelligently. In the Qur'an, Allah says that a believer must not become angry:

> **Those who give in times of both ease and hardship, those who control their rage and pardon other people. Allah loves the good-doers. (Surah Al 'Imran: 134)**

This was also the advice of the Messenger of Allah, may Allah bless him and grant him peace, when he was asked by a man to give him advice and simply said to him: "Do not become angry." (*The Complete Forty Hadith, Imam an-Nawawi*)

Someone who lives according to the teachings of the Qur'an will not change his understanding according to the behaviour of the person he meets. A person may make fun of him, use unpleasant language, get angry, offensive or even aggressive, but a believer's politeness, modesty, mercy and gentleness never change. He doesn't insult a person who insults him first or return ridicule for ridicule, anger for anger. He is calm and controlled if someone is angry with him and will act as our Prophet, may Allah bless him and grant him peace, has advised in one of his hadith:

> "Fear Allah wherever you are, and follow up a bad deed with a good one and it will wipe it out, and behave well towards people." (*Forty Hadith An-Nawawi*)

A believer knows that every moment and every thing is created to test him. For this reason, instead of arguing with someone, he prefers to use good language, and steadfastness to overcome anger directed at him. He knows that this is the kind of behaviour that pleases Allah Whose approval he hopes to win.

# No selfish greed

One of the negative qualities in human nature is selfish greed and Allah tells us in the Qur'an that we must avoid it:

**... But people are prone to selfish greed. If you do good and have taqwa, Allah is aware of what you do. (Surat an-Nisa': 128)**

Some people's selfish greed manifests as envy because others are materially or spiritual superior, or have something they do not. For example, if there is someone more beautiful or attractive, they become envious. Others are envious of people who are rich, successful, knowledgeable, cultured, hard-working or own beautiful houses. Prestige, fame or position can be causes for envy. However, there is one important fact that envious people ignore; and Allah reminds us of it in the Qur'an:

**Or do they in fact envy other people for the bounty Allah has granted them? (Surat an-Nisa': 54)**

Our Lord Allah is the Owner of all things. He provides for anyone He wills and as much as He wills. A human being has no influence over whether more or less is given to him. The Absolute Owner of beauty, property, possessions and superiority is Allah. A believer is aware of this; so no matter what he encounters in the course of a day that he does not own but finds appealing, it will not make him envious. If he sees someone richer or more attractive than himself, he will think of Allah, the only Owner of wealth and beauty. He knows that Allah has chosen what He wills for whom He wills, has given the blessings He wanted to whom He wanted to give them and that the choice and the decision are totally His. The believer acts in a way that acknowledges that Allah has created everything in the best and most beneficial way and that all the various blessings in the world are given to human beings as a test, that the true world is the world to come and that in Allah's presence value is measured in terms of behaviour that pleases Him.

He does not feel selfish greed in sharing the things he owns with others or giving his possessions away. For example, he is not troubled in giving away a favourite possession as a gift or in letting someone else use it. Allah recommends this kind of behaviour to believers in the Qur'an:

**You will not attain true goodness until you give of what you love. Whatever you give away, Allah knows it. (Surah Al 'Imran: 92)**

A believer knows that all the blessings of this earthly life have been given to him only for a while for his use and as a test; he knows that negative traits like selfish greed and envy are wrong.

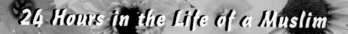

## Avoiding suspicion and gossip

In ignorant society some people have habits that have become inseparable parts of their lives. These are nurturing suspicions about others, prying, or trying to learn private things that don't concern them and slander: gossiping about others and talking behind their backs. These types of behaviour usually go together because someone who slanders someone else does so because they already have unworthy thoughts about him. In the same way, someone who pries into another's business does so because he is suspicious.

In the teachings of the Qur'an there is no room for this kind of unpleasant behaviour and Allah commands believers to avoid it:

**You who believe! Avoid most suspicion. Indeed some suspicion is a crime. And do not spy and do not backbite one another. Would any of you like to eat his brother's dead flesh? No, you would hate it. And have taqwa of Allah. Allah is Ever-Returning, Most Merciful. (Surat al-Hujurat: 12)**

Allah's verses are always in the mind of a believer who carefully avoids behaving in a way that He does not like. He does not try to collect information on another person with an evil intention; He will not say anything unpleasant, anything he is unsure of, or anything that would hurt another's feelings. He will not be caught up in envious surmise on a person about whom he knows nothing. His thoughts about a person he does not know will always be positive; he will speak only about the good and attractive sides of that person. So, taking the example of the reactions of believers to a slander directed at women, Allah says in the Qur'an that a believer who is not sure about the truth of a matter concerning someone else

must think positively about them:

> **Why, when you heard it, did you not, as men and women of the believers, instinctively think good thoughts and say, "This is obviously a lie?" (Surat an-Nur: 12)**

A believer tries always to think positively about his family, friends and those around him, to speak about edifying things and to get others to do the same. But humans are created forgetful as a part of their test in this life and they can make mistakes, but when they become aware of their wrong behaviour, they take refuge in Allah's mercy and ask forgiveness.

## Avoiding sarcasm

A sarcastic attitude is quite widespread among that segment of people who live their lives far from the Qur'an. Among ignorant people, some may ridicule others' shortcomings, mistakes, physical abnormalities, clothing, lack of material possessions, carelessness, behaviour, the way they talk, and in short, almost everything about them. To make fun of someone, they use certain words and gestures or mimic certain facial expressions. For the person making fun, it is not important that he may hurt the other person's feelings, make them sad, annoyed, upset or anxious. The important thing is to feed their own pride and to humiliate the object of their ridicule.

In the Qur'an, Allah definitely forbids people ridiculing others:

**You who believe! People should not ridicule others who may**

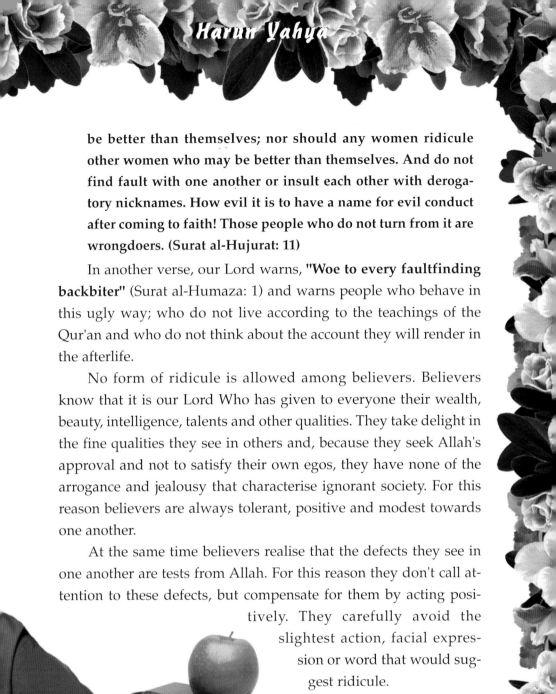

be better than themselves; nor should any women ridicule other women who may be better than themselves. And do not find fault with one another or insult each other with derogatory nicknames. How evil it is to have a name for evil conduct after coming to faith! Those people who do not turn from it are wrongdoers. (Surat al-Hujurat: 11)

In another verse, our Lord warns, **"Woe to every faultfinding backbiter"** (Surat al-Humaza: 1) and warns people who behave in this ugly way; who do not live according to the teachings of the Qur'an and who do not think about the account they will render in the afterlife.

No form of ridicule is allowed among believers. Believers know that it is our Lord Who has given to everyone their wealth, beauty, intelligence, talents and other qualities. They take delight in the fine qualities they see in others and, because they seek Allah's approval and not to satisfy their own egos, they have none of the arrogance and jealousy that characterise ignorant society. For this reason believers are always tolerant, positive and modest towards one another.

At the same time believers realise that the defects they see in one another are tests from Allah. For this reason they don't call attention to these defects, but compensate for them by acting positively. They carefully avoid the slightest action, facial expression or word that would suggest ridicule.

# Self-sacrifice

Those who think that life is restricted to this earthly life do not put themselves out for others unless they stand to get something out of it, and they will not take the initiative to help someone in need. This is because they do not realise that we will receive perfect recompense in the afterlife for the good and the evil we have done in this world. In some verses of the Qur'an, Allah draws our attention to their perverse way of thinking:

**Truly man was created headstrong in greed. (Surat al-Ma'arij: 19)**

**Have you seen him who turns away and gives little, and that grudgingly? (Surat an-Najm: 33-34)**

**As for those who are tight-fisted and direct others to be tight-fisted, and hide the bounty Allah has given them, We have prepared a humiliating punishment for those who disbelieve. (Surat an-Nisa': 37)**

A person must rid himself of the selfishness and meanness of his self. In this regard, our Lord reveals the following:

**So have taqwa of Allah, as much as you are able to, and listen and obey and spend for your own benefit. It is the people who are safe-guarded from the avarice of their own selves who are successful. (Surat at-Taghabun: 16)**

For this reason, a person who lives according to the teachings of the Qur'an will avoid selfishness and make an effort during the day to share what he owns with others around him. For example, he will take pleasure in sharing his food with someone who is hungry. He will happily give prized possessions to someone whose need for them is greater than his own. He will give whatever is surplus to his needs to the needy (Surat al-Baqara: 219). He knows that he will receive a greater reward for it in the afterlife. In the Qur'an, Allah shows us the exemplary behaviour in this regard of the Companions of our Prophet:

**Those who were already settled in the abode, and in faith, before they came, love those who have emigrated to them and do not find in their hearts any need for what they have been given and prefer them to themselves even if they themselves are needy. It is the people who are safeguarded from the avarice of their own selves who are successful. (Surat al-Hashr: 9)**

Believers take delight in the knowledge that their act of self-sacrifice has made someone else happy. They live with the inner peace of mind that comes from acting out of a good conscience and knowing that Allah is pleased. Even when they themselves are in need, they will give up their own rights without a thought. They will never mention their act of self-sacrifice, they will not behave in order to be praised or singled out and they will try to make the other party not feel obliged because of the favour they have done.

# Acting fairly

Believers will not be unaffected by any unfairness they witness, hear or receive indirect information about. The teachings of the Qur'an according to which they live direct them to oppose any kind of cruelty, to defend the rights of those who have been wronged and to intervene on their behalf. In Surat an-Nisa', Allah describes the believers' superior understanding of justice:

**You who believe! Be upholders of justice, bearing witness for Allah alone, even against yourselves or your parents and relatives. Whether they are rich or poor, Allah is well able to look after them. Do not follow your own desires and deviate from the truth. If you twist or turn away, Allah is aware of what you do. (Surat an-Nisa': 135)**

Believers will mobilise all their forces to prevent injustice. Even if most people act in the opposite way, their carelessness and lack of conscience do no make believers lax. They know that they will be questioned in the afterlife about what efforts they made on behalf of justice and what they did to prevent injustice. They will not try to escape their responsibility as very many people do in the world by claiming they did not see, hear or notice anything. They remember that if they act carelessly, not only they are the losers but all the people who are wronged by injustice, and that, if they act conscientiously, not only are they are the winners in the afterlife, but all of the oppressed and wronged people will also benefit. For this reason they will never be disinterested observers of injustice. If there is any injustice at all, they will never ignore it by minding their own business and pretending they haven't seen anything.

Even if the teachings of the Qur'an are in opposition to the profit of the individual human, and even if it is hard to accept, it requires that justice be observed without distinction between mother, father, acquaintance, stranger, rich or poor. For this reason, a believer tries not to commit injustice during the day and strenuously avoids closing his eyes to injustice. He tries to give everyone what they deserve.

For example, when passing in front of people waiting in a queue for a bus, he won't be disrespectful and he will not close his eyes to anyone who does this. He will intervene in a way that is appropriate to noble character and without creating tension. In a contest, he will be careful to praise all those who deserve praise and to receive the award. He will defend those in the right without making any distinction between them and his friends. If he or a close friend makes a mistake, he will openly admit it if the error caused harm to another person and he will do everything in his power to make restitution for the harm done.

## Honesty

Some people see nothing wrong in lying in order to hide a mistake they have made, gain some advantage, save themselves from a difficult situation or to get people to do what they want. Despite the fact that they know what they did is wrong and that their lies may be discovered at any time, they resort to this unpleasant behaviour. They don't remember that they will give an account for everything they have said and done on the Day of Judgment.

But believers never compromise in their honesty. They know that they must be honest at all times, as Allah has revealed in the Qur'an:

> **You who believe! Have taqwa of Allah and speak words which hit the mark [i.e., say what is true and appropriate]. (Surat al-Azhab: 70)**

They obey this command meticulously every day. For example, as we said when discussing an earlier topic, they do not resort to lies to cover up a mistake. They immediately ask for pardon for any mistake they have made and try to make up for it. They do not tell lies in order to gain more respect or to be better liked. No matter what the reason, they do not see lying as a solution.

For this reason, a person who lives according to the teachings of the Qur'an in his daily life does not need to worry about telling a lie or being discovered in a lie. He lives the good, secure and peaceful life that honesty and sincerity bring. Someone who adopts this praiseworthy way of behaviour in this world will receive an even better reward in the afterlife. Allah gives these good tidings to the right-acting:

> **Allah will say, "This is the Day when the truthfulness of the truthful will benefit them. They will have Gardens with rivers flowing under them, remaining in them timelessly, for ever and ever. Allah is pleased with them and they are pleased with Him. That is the Great Victory." (Surat al-Ma'ida: 119)**

# Conclusion

Throughout this book we have seen that believers make it a principle of life twenty-four hours a day to live according to the values that Allah has revealed in the Qur'an. No matter what the conditions, they will not compromise in showing superior behaviour. Their values do not change; they always conform to Allah's commands and recommendations. They take Allah's Messenger, may Allah bless him and grant him peace, as their example whom Allah praises in the Qur'an in these words:

**Indeed you are truly vast in character (Surat al-Qalam: 4)**

There is only one way to escape being lost in the endless punishment of the Fire: living according to the Qur'an and the Sunnah, for by means of these Allah grants to human beings "their Reminder". It saves people from the ignorance in which they are sunk, their primitive way of thinking, stressful environments, negative character traits, baseless fears, perverse beliefs, and the torments of the Fire for which all these things are the causes. In place of these they gain understanding and wisdom, higher values, a sane environment filled with peace of mind and, most importantly,

life in the Garden filled with endless blessings.

There is only one way to remove all the anxiety, battles, wars, hostility, poverty, destitution and anger that fills our world: living according to the teachings of the Qur'an and the Sunnah of Muhammad, may Allah bless him and grant him peace. There is no other way for a person to obtain the happiness, well-being, justice, love and peace that he desires.

Living according to the Qur'an and the Sunnah as a defence against injustice, conflict, inequality, envy, war, unfairness, waste, fear, bigotry, cruelty, violence, immorality and other such things is the most basic solution for human beings in order for them to live at ease, in peace, happiness and justice.

Despite this, and because they have turned their backs on true deen for the sake of small gains, worldly profit and human weakness, some people inflict great harm on themselves. For a human being to turn his back on the Qur'an and Sunnah means that he will remain unaware of truths that are vital for him to know. However, the resources that he and transitory human beings like him have collected will not be enough to survive in the situations and problems that they encounter in the world. People like him will spend their whole lives in anxiety, worry, stress, fear and adversity, with no solution to their problems. And later, they will accept this situation and will spend the rest of their lives deceived, thinking that their suffering is a "fact of life" when it is actually a punishment for not living by the deen.

Believers who follow the values described by Allah in the Qur'an and make them prevail over every moment of their lives will live in the best way. Allah announces good tidings to these believers in the following words:

> It is not your wealth or your children that will bring you near to Us, only in the case of people who believe and act rightly; such people will have a double recompense for what they did. They will be safe from all harm in the High Halls of Paradise. (Surah Saba': 37)

> Those who believe and do right actions and establish prayer and pay zakat, will have their reward with their Lord. They will feel no fear and will know no sorrow. (Surat al-Baqara: 277)

> Those who fulfil Allah's contract and do not break their agreement; those who join what Allah has commanded to be joined and are afraid of their Lord and fear an evil Reckoning; those who are steadfast in seeking the face of their Lord, and establish prayer and give from the provision We have given them, secretly and openly, and stave off evil with good, it is they who will have the Ultimate Abode. (Surat ar-Ra'd: 20-22)

> *They said, "Glory be to You! We have no knowledge except what You have taught us. You are the All-Knowing, the All-Wise." (Surat al-Baqara: 32)*

**WONDERS OF ALLAH'S CREATION**

HARUN YAHYA

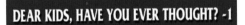

DEAR KIDS, HAVE YOU EVER THOUGHT? -1

**The World of Animals**

HARUN YAHYA

**DEAR KIDS, HAVE YOU EVER THOUGHT? -2**

the glory in the heavens

HARUN YAHYA

**CHILDREN! HAVE YOU EVER THOUGHT? .3.**

Wonderful Creatures

HARUN YAHYA

**DEAR KIDS HAVE YOU EVER THOUGHT? 4**

LET'S LEARN OUR ISLAM

HARUN YAHYA

In the Qur'an, there is an explicit reference to the "second coming of the Jesus to the world." The realization of some information revealed in the Qur'an about Jesus can only be possible by Jesus' second coming...

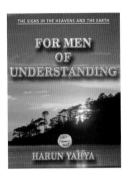

One of the purposes why the Qur'an was revealed is to summon people to think about creation and its works. When a person examines his own body or any other living thing in nature, the world or the whole universe, in it he sees a great design, art, plan and intelligence. All this is evidence proving Allah's being, unit, and eternal power. For Men of Understanding was written to make the reader see and realize some of the evidence of creation in nature. Many living miracles are revealed in the book with hundreds of pictures and brief explanations.

In a body that is made up of atoms, you breathe in air, eat food, and drink liquids that are all composed of atoms. Everything you see is nothing but the result of the collision of electrons of atoms with photons. In this book, the implausibility of the spontaneous formation of an atom, the building-block of everything, living or non-living, is related and the flawless nature of Allah's creation is demonstrated.

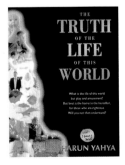

One of the major reasons why people feel a profound sense of attachment to life and cast religion aside is the assumption that life is eternal. However, the world is a temporary place specially created by Allah to test man. That is why, it is inherently flawed and far from satisfying man's endless desires. This book explains this most important essence of life and leads man to ponder the real place to which he belongs, namely the hereafter.

Many societies that rebelled against the will of Allah or regarded His messengers as enemies were wiped off the face of the earth completely... All of them were destroyed—some by a volcanic eruption, some by a disastrous flood, and some by a sand storm...
*Perished Nations* examines these penalties as revealed in the verses of the Quran and in light of archaeological discoveries.

Man is a being to which Allah has granted the faculty of thinking. Yet a majority of people fail to employ this faculty as they should... The purpose of this book is to summon people to think in the way they should and to guide them in their efforts to think.

This book gives an insight into some good moral aspects of the Karma philosophy which are in agreement with the Qur'an, as well as its twisted views which conflict with human reason and conscience. The book also explains why following Allah's way and living by the Qur'an is the only way to real happiness, peace, and security.

For some species, colors serve as a communication tool; for others, they are a warning against enemies. Whatever the case, these colors are essential for the well-being of living beings. An attentive eye would immediately recognize that not only the living beings, but also everything in nature are just as they should be. Furthermore, he would realize that everything is given to the service of man: the comforting blue color of the sky, the colorful view of flowers, the bright green trees and meadows, the moon and stars illuminating the world in pitch darkness together with innumerable beauties surrounding man...

Never plead ignorance of Allah's evident existence, that everything was created by Allah, that you will not stay so long in this world, of the reality of death, that the Qur'an is the Book of truth, that you will give account for your deeds, of the voice of your conscience that always invites you to righteousness, of the existence of the hereafter and the day of account, that hell is the eternal home of severe punishment, and of the reality of fate.

Darwin said: "If it could be demonstrated that any complex organ existed, which could not possibly have been formed by numerous, successive, slight modifications, my theory would absolutely break down." When you read this book, you will see that Darwin's theory has absolutely broken down, just as he feared it would.

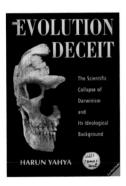

This book clarifies the scientific collapse of the theory of evolution in a way that is detailed but easy to understand. It reveals the frauds and distortions committed by evolutionists to "prove" evolution. Finally it analyzes the powers and motives that strive to keep this theory alive and make people believe in it.
Anyone who wants to learn about the origin of living things, including mankind, needs to read this book.

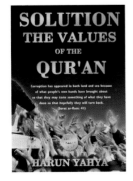

People who are oppressed, who are tortured to death, innocent babies, those who cannot afford even a loaf of bread, who must sleep in tents or even in streets in cold weather, those who are massacred just because they belong to a certain tribe, women, children, and old people who are expelled from their homes because of their religion… Eventually, there is only one solution to the injustice, chaos, terror, massacres, hunger, poverty, and oppression: the morals of the Qur'an.

# Video Films And Audio Cassettes
# Based On The Works Of Harun Yahya

The works of Harun Yahya are also produced in the form of documentary films and cassettes, which are available as VHS, VCD or DVD. This page includes some of these documentaries. Other titles are: Secret Beyond Matter, For Men of Understanding I-II-III, The Miracle in the Ant, The Truth of the Life of This World, Bloody History of Communism I-II-III, The Collapse of Atheism, Islam Denounces Terrorism, Perished Nations I-II, The Secret of the Test, The Names of Allah, Altruism in Nature, Deep Thinking.

Audio presentations based on the works of Harun Yahya are produced in the form of tape-cassettes. The titles in this series include The Theory of Evolution The Fact of Creation, The Creation of the Universe/The Balances in the Earth, The Miracle in the Cell/The Miracle of Birth, The Miracle in the Eye/The Miracle in the Ear, The Design in Animals/The Design in Plants, The Miracle in the Honeybee/The Miracle in the Ant, The Miracle in the Mosquito/The Miracle in the Spider, Self-Sacrifice in Living Things/Migration and Orientation, The Miracle of Creation in DNA, Miracles of the Qur'an.